Paul Galloway

MADE E-Z PRODUCTS, Inc.
Deerfield Beach, Florida / www.MadeE-Z.com

E-Commerce Made E-Z™
Copyright 2000 Made E-Z Products, Inc.
Printed in the United States of America

384 South Military Trail
Deerfield Beach, FL 33442
Tel. 954-480-8933
Fax 954-480-8906
http://www.MadeE-Z.com

1 2 3 4 5 6 7 8 9 10 CPC R 10 9 8 7 6 5 4 3 2

E-Commerce Made E-Z™
Paul Galloway

Limited warranty and disclaimer

This self-help product is intended to be used by the consumer for his/her own benefit. It may not be reproduced in whole or in part, resold or used for commercial purposes without written permission from the publisher. In addition to copyright violations, the unauthorized reproduction and use of this product to benefit a second party may be considered the unauthorized practice of law.

This product is designed to provide authoritative and accurate information in regard to the subject matter covered. However, the accuracy of the information is not guaranteed, as laws and regulations may change or be subject to differing interpretations. Consequently, you may be responsible for following alternative procedures, or using material or forms different from those supplied with this product. It is strongly advised that you examine the laws of your state before acting upon any of the material contained in this product.

As with any matter, common sense should determine whether you need the assistance of an attorney. We urge you to consult with an attorney, qualified estate planner, or tax professional, or to seek any other relevant expert advice whenever substantial sums of money are involved, you doubt the suitability of the product you have purchased, or if there is anything about the product that you do not understand including its adequacy to protect you. Even if you are completely satisfied with this product, we encourage you to have your attorney review it.

Neither the author, publisher, distributor nor retailer are engaged in rendering legal, accounting or other professional services. Accordingly, the publisher, author, distributor and retailer shall have neither liability nor responsibility to any party for any loss or damage caused or alleged to be caused by the use of this product.

Copyright Notice

Table of contents

Introduction to E-Commerce Made E-Z™

The purpose of this guide is to show you how to use the newest technology tools to sell more of your products and/or services. We are in an information age—and when people want information about your product, they want it RIGHT NOW. If you fail to fill your prospect's desire for instant gratification, that prospect goes to someone else who will. Why not? It's only a mouse click or telephone call away! Your challenge is to capture the prospect's attention, arouse their desire, and show them how to get what they want, how to solve their problems—RIGHT NOW—by getting your product or service!

The new tools we discuss will help you to meet that challenge in three ways:

1) *Marketing research and testing*: Using these tools, you can home in on your target market, find out what their "hot buttons" are, and test/tune your marketing messages in a fraction of the time it would take using conventional methods alone.

2) *Customer feedback*: These tools make possible frequent, cheap, and FAST communications between you and your customers, including invaluable customer feedback that you otherwise never get.

3) *Customer convenience*. Make things easy for your customers, and fast too. With these tools, your customer can get information about your product or service immediately, and based on that information can place an order (in various ways) 24 hours a day. And, it won't cost you an arm and a leg to provide this convenience!

Some of these tools have been around a longer than others, but had prices that put them out of reach of some of us small operators. So, in addition to discussing the tools themselves, I recommend some of the inexpensive sources for them. The wise use of this new technology can put you on equal footing with many of the large companies.

Though these tools ARE powerful, they are not meant to be used by themselves. They work best—rather, they ONLY WORK—when you use them in conjunction with conventional methods of promoting your business. Simply put, these tools are extensions or enhancements of long-practiced and proven direct marketing methods. Use them and you decrease the costs and the time required to develop, test and "tweak" your various direct marketing messages.

While they lend themselves especially well to the information marketer, these tools can also be adapted quite easily to the storefront business (in fact, storefront business owners may enjoy some advantages over the home-based operator, and these advantages should be exploited). Several people in "traditional" businesses (such as carpet cleaning and financial planning) used direct marketing techniques to propel them far beyond the income levels of others in their fields. You can do this too, and the new tools we discuss in this guide make it even easier for you to get started—with much lower risk.

This guide is divided into five chapters. The first chapter consists of fundamentals of direct marketing—things like developing your USP, principles of targeted marketing, and basics of creating your sales messages. The discussions in the following chapters assume your familiarity with these fundamentals, so if you are just starting out in direct marketing or if you need a little primer, this chapter is for you!

Chapter Two is where I talk about the tools themselves—what they are, how they work, and how they can be of use to you in building your business!

The third chapter is a review of the various direct marketing methods these tools can be used with. Internet marketing is also discussed in this chapter.

Chapter Four is made up entirely of references and resources. It contains the contact information for services and products of use to the small/home business owner—including the companies/tools discussed in Chapter Two. It also includes book references and other reference material of interest to the direct marketer.

Chapter Five talks about getting free publicity, and after that I included a bonus report about simple methods to conduct critical marketing research—doing this could be the difference between the success and failure of your current project, so be sure to read the report!

P. Galloway

Fundamentals of direct marketing

1

Chapter 1

Fundamentals of direct marketing

What you'll find in this chapter:

- Finding your Unique Selling Proposition (USP)
- Defining your market
- Why you need a "swipe" file
- The power of good copywriting
- Turning failure into success

While the discussions in later chapters require a basic understanding of these fundamental principles of direct marketing, this chapter is NOT an exhaustive or thorough treatment of these principles by any means! If you really want to be successful in direct marketing you should study the direct marketing books I listed in Chapter Four—you would do well to read them all!

Even the most acknowledged experts in the field of direct marketing make a habit of continually learning and studying their trade—if THEY do it, how much more so should you and I! Start modeling your success by following their example of constant learning.

PRELIMINARIES

Define your USP

Before you do ANY marketing, you need to have a clear understanding of what your *Unique Selling Proposition (USP)* is. Some marketers prefer to call this their unique selling Position or Advantage, but it all means the same thing.

Your *USP* is what sets you apart from all the other companies selling similar products. It's the strongest benefit for your customer. If someone asked you "Why should I buy from YOU instead of Company X?" Your answer would be the USP for your company. The ideal situation would be for you to have a highly desirable product that no one else had—just having the product would be your USP. Unfortunately, you'll rarely be in this enviable situation—you may have a product that no one else offers at first, but if you have any success you will soon have some fierce competition!

What are some other (more realistic) possibilities for a USP? Here are just a few:

- **Lowest Price.** This is probably the one most people think of first, and it is one of the most used USPs—though most people that use it don't even know what a USP is! Several stores have put a twist on this USP: "If you can find it for less money anywhere else, we'll pay you double the difference."

  Perhaps you have the lowest price because you are the originator of the product and everyone else

> *note* If you use the low price USP, be sure to address the natural (and usually unspoken) concern that low price corresponds to low quality.

is paying you licensing fees. Or, you just deal in such large volume that you get major cost breaks. Let people know there is a good reason that you can sell it for less money, *and* still maintain the quality.

One more thing to be careful of . . . don't cut your price so much for this USP that you have too little margin! If you can't profitably cut your price enough to have the "lowest price" USP, then use a different USP—there are many, and price is not always the most important thing to your potential customers!

- **Satisfaction Guarantee.** If you offer a strong enough guarantee you can use that as your USP. For instance, how many new car dealers offer to buy your car back from you anytime within 60 days of purchase if you decide you don't like it? I have yet to see anyone advertising that where I live!

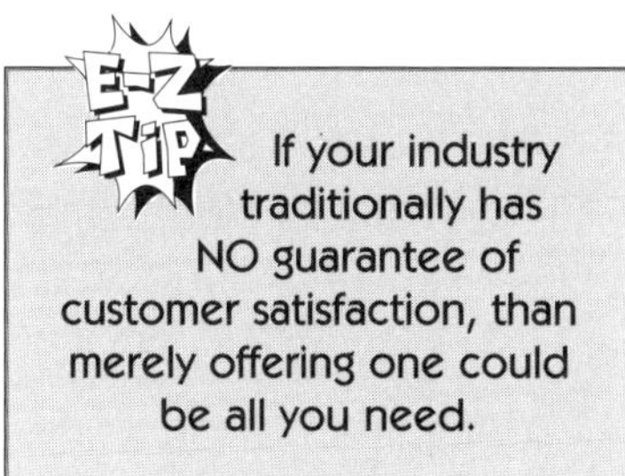

In most industries, however, a satisfaction guarantee is expected, so yours needs to be exceptional if you are going to make it your USP. Something like a 150% money back guarantee . . . however, if you offer something like that, your product/service better deliver!

One good example of a strong guarantee is the one used by "The CLUB"—the car theft deterrent that you lock on your car's steering wheel. They offer to pay your deductible if your car is ever stolen while their product is in use. Some computer "surge protection" devices come with a guarantee that if your equipment is ever damaged while the surge protector is in place, they replace your equipment—up to $25,000 worth! This could easily be the USP of the company selling the device.

- **Quality.** Sure, everyone claims to have good quality. But, if you can demonstrate specific and verifiable reasons why your product is superior to everyone else's, you can make this your USP.

- **After-Sale Service.** Whether it's on-site training, toll-free computer software support, or 12 months of free preventative maintenance on your car (oil change, tire rotation, etc.), after-sale service is a big deal to your customers. If it's good enough, it may be the best benefit you offer your customer, and a great USP!

- **Payment terms.** If you offer 90 days same as cash, your own "in-store credit," or other flexible payment plans, that may be enough to sway customers' opinions in your favor.

- **Freebies/Premiums.** If you give something away with every order, this adds value to your product. The higher the perceived value of your premium, the more successful you'll be using it as your USP. Good examples are the various health and financial newsletters—most of them offer a free book with your 1 or 2 year subscription. In fact, some of their sales materials talk more about the free book than the newsletter!

Look at your product and company—what is it that you excel at? What is the best benefit you offer your customers? THAT is your USP! Or, look at all your competition. What benefits do they offer? Are there any benefits they DON'T offer—perhaps a benefit your research shows is highly desired by the marketplace? If so, you just offer that benefit yourself and let that benefit be your USP!

> *note* Other USPs might include availability, expertise, size, customization, free shipping, distribution channels, more choices, and many others.

Though it is called a unique selling proposition, that doesn't mean that it must be something no one else is doing. That is the ideal, yes, but let's face it, there are some industries where everyone pretty much does business the same way. I personally think that with some creativity you could change that . . . you could add bonuses, do SOMETHING to add to the value of your offer.

E-Z TIP Even if everyone else in your field or industry is doing the same thing, you can emphasize a particular thing, and make it YOURS.

Just for the sake of argument, let's pretend that you do business the same way as everyone else—you buy from the same supplier, you offer the same prices, support, service . . . everything is the same. You can still have a highly marketable USP!

As an example, look at Dunkin' Donuts. Do you remember the commercial showing the baker struggling to get out of bed early in the morning because he has to "make the donuts?" The BENEFIT to the customer was that they got warm, freshly baked donuts every morning. Do you think Dunkin' Donuts is the only donut franchise where someone has to get up early (in time for the pre-workday business)? Of course not! Everyone in the donut business does that! But, guess who owns that particular USP (donuts baked fresh every morning) until the end of time? Dunkin' Donuts, of course!

CAUTION Don't make the mistake of copying someone else's USP—it makes you look bad, and just won't work!

note

No donut company is going to advertise "Hey, we bake our donuts early every morning too!"—*there is no room for "me too" with a USP*—whoever stakes their claim to a particular USP in their industry or marketplace owns it forever, as long as they fulfill their promises associated with it! Other donut companies have to come up with their own USP (how about "Free coffee with any morning visit!").

So, what do you do once you determine what your USP is? What the heck good does it do you? Why is the USP so important? Because it helps you to focus on the greatest benefit you offer. If your customers and potential customers are exposed over and over to this USP, they soon associate that particular benefit with your company. It won't matter if other companies copy that benefit later, the public perception is that YOU have the monopoly on that benefit—and if it's a strong enough benefit, they will want to deal with you exclusively . . . that's the goal, now, isn't it?!

Once you know what your USP is, you must make it a part of all your advertisements and sales letters—in fact, you must make it a part of everything you do! When you acknowledge your customers orders, send them a refund, ask them to fill out a marketing survey, thank them for their business, or at any other time that you deal with your customers, your USP should be an integral part of your communication.

> CAUTION
> Make sure the USP you develop and promote is one you can make good on every time!

Not only that, but you should make it a part of every facet of your business. Share your USP with your staff (in fact, you may want their help in developing it), explain to them what it means and how you'll give that promised benefit to your customers. When they answer the phone, send a letter, or in any other way deal with your customers or potential customers, they must have this USP in their mind.

One final word of caution here. Once you establish a USP, you "walk the razors edge"—fail to fulfill that promised benefit, and you can kiss that USP good-bye in the eyes of your customers or potential customers.

When you promote your USP as you should, the distinction between that benefit and your company is lost . . . so if the benefit (USP) is not REAL, your company may as well not be real either, as far as the customer is concerned. You simply cannot stay in business with that kind of customer sentiment!

Define your market

As a small or home business owner you can't afford the image advertising approach used by the large corporations. You must have a narrowly defined niche market that you can focus your efforts upon.

For instance, consider a large grocery store chain. Everyone must eat . . . their "target market" is "everyone within a 10 mile radius." So, they advertise on TV and Radio, in the newspaper, and through weekly flyers in the mail. They blanket an area with advertising, and it's very expensive, but it's the only way they can do business.

> **note** The broader your market, the more money you have to spend to generate new customers.

Now compare this to a mortgage company offering home mortgage refinancing. The first thing they can do is cross off anyone on their "potential client list" that is not a homeowner. Then they can eliminate anyone whose mortgage is too small or whose current interest rate is too low to benefit from refinancing. They probably would prefer to deal only with "creditworthy" clients, further narrowing their market. For matters of customer convenience, they decide to limit their efforts to a geographic area within a 10 minute drive from their office.

Their target market is then be defined as "credit worthy homeowners within these boundaries (pointing to a map) and having a mortgage of $80,000 or more with an interest rate of 9.5% or higher." How much less expensive it would be to reach this target market.

Since mortgage details are a matter of public record, the mortgage company could find all the names and addresses of homeowners meeting their "target market definition." Instead of wasting money by advertising to everyone (including those who have no use for their service), they can focus all their attention on the defined market.

Instead of mailing 50,000 letters once, they can mail a series of seven letters to 3,000 homeowners—personalized and customized sales letters, I might add! And they can follow up on those sales letters with phone calls. All this attention focused on the people who can really BENEFIT from their service, and at much less than the cost of advertising to a less defined audience.

What factors determine your target market? Here are a few obvious ones:

- age
- gender
- income level
- have a credit card?
- hobbies
- education
- homeowner?
- type of job

Another very important factor (especially when looking for relevant mailing lists) is if they bought items similar to yours before and what they paid for them.

If you have customers already, the best way to find out who your target market is to send them a survey or questionnaire. Find out what kind of person is buying your product already. You should also use this opportunity to get some feedback from the customer on your product—you should ALWAYS do this!

See the special bonus report that comes with this guide *The dirty little secret about market research that no one ever talks about.* It gives the basics of how to conduct simple and quick marketing research.

The grocery store and mortgage company comparison above was an example from a local perspective. Suppose you are marketing something nationally. You are in luck! Chances are there are magazines, newsletters, trade journals, weekly papers, or some other kind of periodical that appeals to your target market. There are also thousands of mailing lists. Once you know your target market, you can home in on them with the SRDS resources (you can read more about this in Chapters Three and Four).

Create your own "swipe" file

If you are going to be successful at promoting your business through direct marketing and e-commerce, you need to be intimately familiar with the methods that are working for OTHER direct marketers.

Why? Because your best chance for success is to do the same things that proved successful for others! As a small business owner, you don't have the luxury of risking hundreds or thousands of dollars on a "new and revolutionary idea" for promotion. You need to stick with the methods that are proven to work for others.

I know, I know, there are many examples of people who were wildly successful by breaking all the rules. There are always exceptions, but the odds are much more in your favor if you model the successes of others. You may get tired of hearing me say this, because I will say it over and over again . . . be warned!

> *note*
> Once a large franchise chain has chosen a particular location, all the others take advantage of the many research dollars spent by their competitor, and quickly set up their own operations on adjacent lots.

It goes against everyone's fantasy of being extraordinarily successful while thumbing your nose at all the "boring" traditional/conventional methods . . . but look, even the fast food giants do it! Ever notice how once you have a McDonald's at a particular location, it is soon followed by a Burger King and/or Wendy's and/or Arby's and/or . . . ???? These restaurants copy each other, just like you should copy the successful methods of your competitors and business peers!

DEFINITION

A *swipe file* is a resource for you to use whenever you write your own sales messages—a collection of other copywriters' work that you can use to "swipe" ideas from. Hang on now, I am not suggesting that you copy any advertisement or sales letter (or even a sentence from a sales letter) word for word.

When you see an advertisement that really catches your eye . . . one that draws you in, holds you in a vise, makes you ache for the advertised product, and makes you immediately pick up the phone and order . . . it would be a great model to use for your own ad ideas, don't you agree? You should subscribe to every periodical or industry journal related to the product you are selling . . . and when you see a good ad, you should file it in your swipe file.

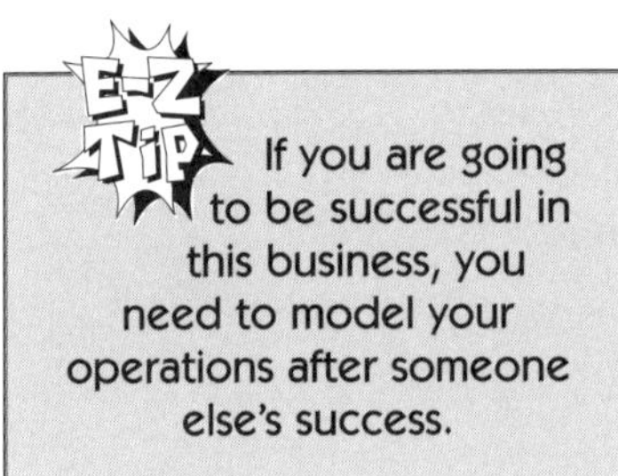

Now, perhaps you see an ad that doesn't really pull you in—perhaps you're just not interested in what they're selling. But, if that ad continues to run week after week, month after month, you can bet it is a successful ad and you can learn something from it! You may want to copy the concept behind the headline, or maybe it is the guarantee that is so powerful . . . or the testimonials that build up the credibility of the message. When you set out to create your own sales message, your job is much easier—and your odds at success are much greater—if you model it after others that proved successful.

> note
>
> Your efforts to model others' success should not end with your advertisements or sales letters. You should examine every aspect of a successful company's operation.

Find out where they advertise, how they respond to inquiries. Analyze their sales letters and phone scripts. Call their order line and pay attention to how their operators are trained. Do they offer an "upsell" option? Order their product and see how good it is, what it's features and benefits are. See how they handle their customers after the sale. Get the idea?

In short, you want to know what everyone (who is successful) is doing, and then do the same thing, only better!

> **note** Even if you already know that your product is of superior quality and costs less, you still need to study your competitors.

The most valuable information you'll get from doing this will be from companies selling the same kind of product or service as you—yes, that's right, your competitors. You better know what they are doing, if no one else! You need to make your offer better than theirs, and how can you do that if you aren't familiar with their operation? Perhaps their USP (see Chapter One) has nothing to do with quality or price. Maybe people buy from them because of their after-sales support. If you don't know, they could roll right over you, and you would never know what went wrong.

COPYWRITING

The most powerful tool of all

So, you have your own business, and you want to increase your sales through direct marketing and e-commerce. Being the smart business person that you are, you want to use FAX, Fax-On-Demand, E-mail, Autoresponders, Inbound Telemarketing, Voice Mail, Interactive Voice Mail, and various Internet-based tools. In short, you want to use every tool at your disposal.

However, before you get too carried away with all these marvels of technology, there is one tool—an old tool that predates just about every other—that you MUST master if you are to be successful. Ineffective use of this one tool renders all other tools USELESS! What is this tool? As you may have guessed, I am talking about:

THE WRITTEN WORD!

That's write (oops, I mean "right"!), and I'm sure you're saying "I knew that!"

I'm not trying to be clever here, I'm very serious. If you are to make a success of your business through direct marketing and e-commerce, you MUST learn how to use words. No matter how many different ways you deliver them, if your words do not give your prospects the motivation to purchase your product or service, your marketing will fall flat on its face.

The art (or science, depending on who you're talking to) of using words to get sales is often referred to as *copywriting*. Several books were written on this one subject, and some of the better ones are given in the references/resources chapter (Chapter Four) of this guide. While a thorough treatment of copywriting techniques is beyond the scope of this guide, I show you the BASICS of copywriting and trust that you'll study some of the recommended materials **before** your first copywriting venture.

note

When it comes down to successful marketing, words are your most powerful tools, PERIOD.

The first thing you should understand about copywriting is that YOU are trying to control your readers, **through their emotions**, long enough to move them to some action. Usually we think of that action as placing an order, but it could also be the action of requesting more information, calling for a consultation appointment, or some other action that is intended to be a precursor to the actual sale of your product or service.

Notice the bold face words above? I want to emphasize that copywriting is a game of emotions. How did you feel when you read the word "manipulating?" I KNOW that some people will read that word and feel a pang of guilt. "Manipulation" has such a negative connotation. That's okay, no need to feel guilty, so long as you are selling something that truly benefits your customers.

> **note**
>
> If your direct marketing sales messages are to be successful, it will only be by manipulating the readers' emotions, appealing to their basic emotional fears and desires.

One of the books which I highly recommend is Herschell Gordon Lewis's *Direct Mail Copy That Sells!* Here is a quote from that book about copywriting:

> *WHEN EMOTION AND INTELLECT COME INTO CONFLICT, EMOTION ALWAYS WINS.*
>
> *As unyielding as that rule is, I'll stick to it with no qualifiers, no "except . . .," no "if you . . ." or, "but you must . . ." followers. The rule stands, Gibraltar on the stormy seas of I-guess-this-should-work direct response copywriting.*
>
> *. . . our job is to interfere with the reader's natural skepticism and force that person—our subject—to lift a pen or the phone and respond to our message.*

Having said this, it is important for you to understand just what emotions motivate people to take action. Generally, the recognized motivators—the only reasons that people do anything—(in no particular order) are:

- Fear
- Greed
- Guilt
- Exclusivity/Pride
- Love

Let's just briefly go over each one of these.

Fear

Of all the weapons in the marketer's arsenal, fear is the most powerful. People fear losing their investments, their jobs, or their health. We fear rejection, "missing out," losing face, or just plain failing. We fear for the safety of our families. Quoting Lewis again (last time I promise—but you really should get his book!):

> note
> People will act out of fear for losing what they have before they will act out of greed for more.

In a skilled surgeon's hands, Fear cuts through the layers of fat around the reader's brain, jabbing and needling until, trembling with the unquenchable desire built on frustration, the recipient of your Fear message grabs his pen or his phone to soothe his fever.

Greed

My dictionary defines greed as "acquisitive or selfish desire beyond reason." When we think of a greedy person, we usually think of someone like Charles Dickens' Scrooge. People like that probably do exist (I say probably because I've never met one myself), but most people are much better than that! No, the greed we talk about here is not necessarily bad. It's just the natural tendency to want something more than what we have now, be it more money, more free time, more vacations, a nicer car, or better clothing. Sometimes it will be about getting something for less—that's what a sale is all about!

Guilt

Guilt can also be a powerful emotion. As one ancient religious leader once wrote: ". . . the guilty taketh the truth to be hard, for it cutteth them to the very center."

Everyone has ideas of what they should do, what kind of person they should be, what is right and what is wrong—and sometimes when we cross the "right/wrong" line, we try to buy redemption in the form of flowers, candy, an apologetic card, or any number of other things. Many nonprofit organizations use guilt as their main marketing tool by making their prospects feel guilty about not contributing to their most-worthy cause ("What kind of person are you if you won't even spend $25 to feed these starving children?").

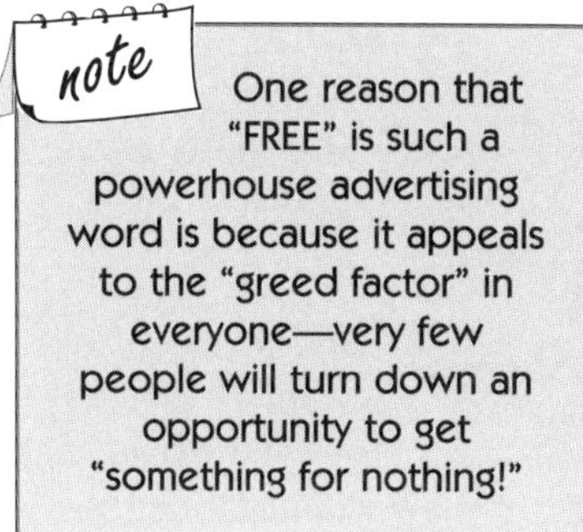

Pride/Exclusivity

Everyone has at one time or another fantasized of being extraordinary at something, impressing everyone around them, having everyone look up at them with awe. People want to be seen by those around them as important, and they will go to great lengths (and expense) to project that image. Exclusivity is something that goes hand-in-hand with pride. If there are only certain people who are eligible for the honor of spending $25,000 for a golf club membership, well then, they must be important, right? (Never mind that the only qualifier is that they *have* the $25,000 to spend!)

This headline makes good use of the pride/exclusivity motivator: "They grinned when the waiter spoke to me in French, but their laughter changed to amazement at my reply." What a masterful way of painting a picture with words!

As you read that headline, you can actually picture yourself sitting at a fine French restaurant, and replying to the waiter in fluent French. You can further imagine—just from reading this one headline—all your friends exchanging looks of shock and amazement. Further, you can imagine them all speaking up at once, saying things like, "I didn't know you spoke French!" "How did you learn?" "That was great, say something else in French!"

As an aside, did you notice the headline borrows heavily from the classic *They Laughed When I Sat Down At the Piano...But When I Started To Play!*—the words are different, but the concept is precisely the same. This type of headline has been used countless times!

Love

Love and romance, the cornerstone of the Greeting Card industry! Call me sentimental and naive, but I'm a firm believer that there is no power greater than love. However, in the marketing arena, fear and greed proved to be better motivators.

Be that as it may, there will always be people who, despite the old saying "you can't buy love," spend handsome sums to delight their loved ones. The natural things to think of are jewelry, fine china, cards, relationship books—that kind of thing. But, you could also use the emotion of love to promote vacations, portraits, and insurance, couldn't you? Or, how about a reminder service (never forget your anniversary again!), or a surprise party service? There are all kinds of possibilities!

Lead with benefits, follow with features

There is one more concept I'd like to go over before I go into the specifics of copywriting—the difference between features and benefits. In the earlier discussion about defining your USP, I talked about using your biggest benefit to the customer as your USP. Sometimes, though, people confuse benefits with features.

To illustrate the differences, consider someone selling a car-towing service. I just picked up my yellow pages and the first thing I saw was the towing listings. In one advertisement, I saw the following words: *'24-Hour Towing. Radio Dispatched. Fort Lauderdale Terminals. Flat Bed."* All of these are features—not BENEFITS!

A *feature* is a fact about your product or service. Things like size, color, contents, availability, location . . . these are all "features." The advantages the customer enjoys as a result of those features is a benefit. One simple way to convert features to benefits is to ask yourself "What is the advantage this feature gives my customer?" Another way is to put yourself in the position of talking to your customer. Talk to them and say "You get . . ." or "You will . . ." In the case of the features "Radio Dispatched" and "24 Hour Towing" the advantage (spoken to the customer) is "You will be taken care of within 15 minutes."

> **note** That doesn't mean that features can't be a part of your message—you NEED features to give credibility to your claimed benefits.

The benefits hit the emotional buttons of your prospect, and the features support those benefits. How about: "You will be taken care of within 15 minutes of calling—our 24 hour on-call radio dispatched trucks will insure that!" In this case your features are used to explain how it is possible for your customer to receive the advertised "benefit." You get the idea.

First, tell your customer how they will benefit (emotion). Then, back that claim up with facts (logic). This is where the old copywriting adage "Lead with benefits, follow with features" comes from. Use it and profit!

Using the AIDA formula

Finally, we're ready to discuss the format of the advertisement itself. The classic formula for writing advertisements and sales letters is *AIDA*, which stands for "Attention, Interest, Desire, Action." To that classic formula, add the letters *EQ*, for "Easy" and "Quickly." Let's examine these one by one:

Attention

The first thing you must do is get your prospect's ATTENTION. This is usually done with the headline of your sales letter or advertisement. Many copywriters maintain that you must spend 80% to 90% of your copywriting efforts on the headline alone! In his book *Magic Words That Bring You Riches,* Ted Nicholas quoted John Caples (author of *Making Ads Pay* and the man who created the headline "They Laughed When I Sat Down At the Piano...But When I Started To Play!"):

> *Advice to copywriters: When you are assigned to write an ad, write a lot of headlines first. Spend hours writing headlines—or days if necessary. If you happen to think of a headline while walking down the street or while riding the bus, take out a pencil and paper and write it down.*

Besides getting attention, your headline should highlight your most powerful benefit, and can also be used to qualify or select your target audience. By this I mean that if your offer is targeted towards retirees, you should have something in the headline that appeals especially to retirees. This CAN be obvious—"*Free report for retirees only: How to THRIVE on $10 per day!"*—nothing wrong with that! John Caples' piano headline was more subtle, but served to select an audience of people interested in discovering how to play the piano.

> note
>
> The headline is the most read part of any sales letter or advertisement, and this is where you need to spend most of your time.

This is when your swipe file comes in handy. Examining the headlines used successfully by others may give you some good ideas about your own headlines. It's also a good idea to read through all the publications related to the product or service you're selling. Sometimes the articles themselves have headlines that are easily adaptable to a successful advertisement headline.

After you studied the subject matter, start writing your own headlines. Write down every benefit your product or service offers your customers, and make a headline using each of these. Then do combinations.

note

Each headline should be able to stand on its own. In other words, the headline by itself should be enough to get people to ask for more information if it were used as a classified ad. You've seen the headlines that simply say "STOP!"—well, they wouldn't pass this test. Who would ask for more information upon seeing a classified ad saying:

> note
>
> Try to get into the mind of your customers, see what they are thinking.

"STOP! Call 555-555-5555 (recording) for free report!"

Ridiculous, isn't it? Now how about this one:

"Free report for retirees only: How to THRIVE on $10 per day! Call 555-555-5555 (recording) for free report!"

When Ted Nicholas is working on an ad, he sometimes writes as many as 250 different headlines before deciding which one to use. His ads were responsible for over ½ BILLION dollars in sales, so I would say his is a good example to emulate, wouldn't you agree? It takes time, but believe me, it is worth it! Refer to the Reference/Resources Chapter for a list of the generally accepted power words that you should include in your headline.

> note
>
> Make sure that your headline is enticing enough that someone would want more information even if the headline was the ONLY thing they were able to read.

Interest

Next, you must capture their INTEREST. Assuming your headline is enough to get the reader to pause and look at your ad, your sub-headlines and first couple of paragraphs must be engaging enough to hook your readers and get them to read the rest of your message. If you wrote several alternate headlines before choosing one for your ad, you should have several others that are almost as good. Use these as sub-headlines. Hit your prospect with benefit, benefit, benefit—not features!

Desire

Now your task becomes that of arousing DESIRE in your prospect—desire for the benefits of your product or service. Desire for the solution—which you offer—to their problem. You need to make them feel the pain that not having your product or service is causing them, and show them that your product/service will ease that pain! You need to amplify the fear, greed, or other motivator you used in your headline.

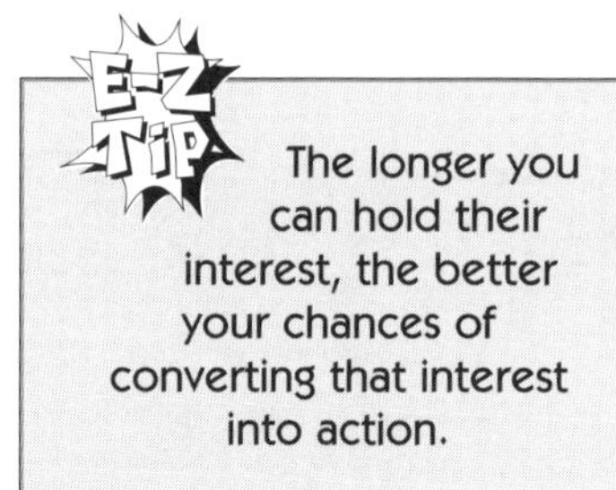

If you're using fear as your motivator, remind them of the danger they are in—not necessarily PHYSICAL danger (unless you're selling some kind of anti-crime or safety device)—I'm talking about the danger of missing out on an opportunity, staying in the same old rut, not being successful, not being respected or liked, or whatever it is that your product/service will help them overcome.

If you're using greed as the motivator, remind them of the money they could save, or the money they could make. You get the idea . . . this is where you reinforce the fear/greed/etc. that your headline first drew your prospect's attention to.

This is where you seize control of your prospect's mind, and make them believe that the only way out of this mess, the only way to improve their lot in life is to have what you are offering! Before they reach the "action" section of your sales message, they should be saying to themselves "I MUST HAVE THIS!"

Action

Finally, you must move your prospect to ACTION. Get them to call in, mail, fax, e-mail, or telegraph you their order (or a request for additional information, if that's the goal of your sales message). You must tell them exactly what to do: "Fill in the coupon below and send or fax to . . . or call 1-800-555-5555 with your credit card number."

Make it easy for them to order—I know for a fact that there were times I was ready to place an order for a book, and there was no phone number to call for placing the order. The sales letter and order coupon got tossed in the trash—I don't want to mess with mailing an order. I wanted the book enough to part with $40, but not enough to go through the effort of:

1) Finding and addressing an envelope
2) Filling out the order coupon
3) Finding and affixing a stamp
4) Taking the envelope to the mailbox

Plus, I didn't like the additional time I would have to wait for the U.S. Postal Service to deliver my order. If I could have called or faxed the order in, I would have—in my case, the book was worth the money, but not worth the aggravation of placing the order by mail.

Perhaps I'm lazier than most, but I'm sure I wasn't the only one who tossed that particular sales letter in the trash because of the lack of a more convenient ordering mechanism!

Besides making it easy to order, you must give the prospect a reason to take action NOW. This reason could be because you have limited quantities, or because you only have a certain number of free bonuses to give away with orders. Or, perhaps you are just going to reward them for ordering within a certain period of time by cutting the price by 50% (I see this tactic being used all the time). If you have a time limit, it is better to specify a DATE, rather than a given number of days.

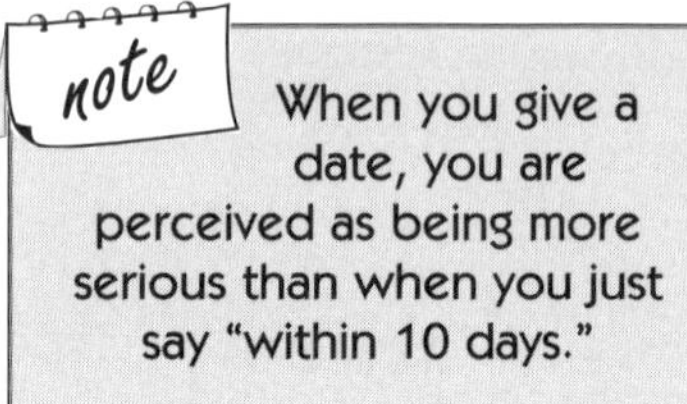

When you give a date, you are perceived as being more serious than when you just say "within 10 days."

General recommendations

Now that you know about the basic concepts behind AIDA, here are a few general recommendations about your advertisements and sales letters. These are generalities. There are always exceptions to the rule—but until you read several books on copywriting techniques and/or have some experience behind you, you're safer sticking with the tried-and-true methods.

- ***Know the GOAL of your sales message:*** Before you start your sales letter or advertisement, have a clear idea of exactly what the goal of that message is. You either want the prospect to place an order, or request more information, or perhaps a consultation . . . whatever it is, you must know what the sales message is supposed to accomplish before you start writing! To make sure they achieve this clarity, some copywriters design the ordering coupon first.

- ***Write simple:*** Some people write to look smart. Don't. The only way to measure "smarts" in this business is with net

Remember, if someone must stop to figure out what you're saying, you have LOST THEM!

income. If you want people to BUY, you write so they understand you! To start off, just write as if you were writing a friend. Use common language—just like when you talk—not the formal language taught in school. Use small paragraphs, small sentences, and small words. You may even want to start simply by recording yourself as you describe the benefits of the product or service you're offering. People like to read in small segments. If they see a huge, unbroken paragraph, they think of reading it as a task. I'm not saying never use a word that has more than two syllables . . . as long as you use words your recipients consider everyday language, you are fine.

- ***Use emotional words:*** This is really just an extension of write simple. Instead of intellectual words, use simpler words—words that people readily understand and don't have to translate (subconsciously, but translate nonetheless) to simpler terms. You just want them to follow along smoothly and happily as you lead them to the emotional decision (I WANT IT!) to get what you are offering. Make your message such that a fourth grader can read it without stumbling over the words. Go through your sales message once you've written it, and if you find any words that can be replaced with simpler, easily understood words, then do it!

> *note* You don't want to bring people to an intellectual plane—you DON'T want them to analyze anything.

Most word processors now have a grammar checking utility built in. After going through your document, it tells you the reading difficulty level of your writing—aim for a fourth grade equivalent difficulty.

- ***Use "YOU" writing, not "ME" writing:*** The first mistake most inexperienced copywriters make is writing about the company making the offer. What's the first thing you see on many sales letter? The company letterhead! That's NOT "you" advertising, it's "me" advertising. The customer doesn't care one iota about your company, how long it's been in business, how big it is, or how many dollars in annual sales you did last year.

  What the customer wants to know is simply "What's in it for me?"—your sales letter should be filled with words like "you," you're," "your," "you'll"—notice a pattern here?

  You need to talk about the person reading your sales message, show him how he benefits from the product or service you're offering. If there is a true benefit associated with the fact that you're the biggest company in your field, then show the reader that benefit, and validate your claim with the facts behind it.

- ***Always include a strong guarantee:*** People these days are skeptical—extremely skeptical! This being the case, you need a strong guarantee. The reader wants to know that they have no risk at all, that you will cheerfully refund their money for any reason whatsoever. Basically, they want a NO RISK deal, and if you want their business, you better give it to them!

> E-Z TIP: If there is no associated benefit, the facts won't help you sell. Remember, you sell with benefits (emotion), not features (logic/facts)!

Certainly, one of the strongest guarantees I've seen is having a "Postage Paid" return label included as part of the sales message. The reader is told, "Look, we're giving you this postage paid return label. If you aren't 100% satisfied with this book in every way, just put it back in the box, slap this label on it, and drop it in the mail! We'll send you a refund immediately!"

In the earlier discussion of developing your USP, I shared a couple of other strong guarantees—there are many different ways of using the guarantee to reassure the prospect that YOU are taking all the risk. Make sure you do it!

- ***Use testimonials:*** The best way to convince your readers that your benefits are real is to have testimonials from previous customers backing up your claims. Try to think of every possible objection or fear that the customer may have about your offer. Then use a testimonial that addresses that specific issue. Don't use testimonials like "Your (product) is great!," or even "Worth every penny!" Use testimonials like this:

note

Your guarantee must convince the reader of your sales message that when they accept your offer, YOU will be the only one assuming any risk.

> "(Product Name) has already saved me $342 and I've only had it for two weeks!"
>
> *A. Franklin, Albany NY*

> "I was skeptical when I ordered your book, but was pleasantly surprised when it arrived two days later! Using the techniques you shared in your book, I have increased my weekly profits by 36% in less than 30 days!"
>
> *R. Howard, Wichita, KS*

See the difference? These testimonials address specific issues (effectiveness of the product, quick delivery). If you have a specific testimonial that addresses every possible customer objection, you'll do very, *very* well!

- ***Read it out loud:*** Once your first draft is done, read it out loud. Any point where you stumble in your reading needs to be changed until you can read through it smoothly.

- ***Take time to cool off:*** When you feel that your sales message is finished, put it away somewhere and leave it alone for a minimum of a day, and preferably a week. Let the whole thing bounce around in your subconscious for awhile, and then come back to it. You'll probably see things that could be improved.

- ***Write for two types of people:*** There are impulsive people who scan an ad and if they like what they see, order—even without reading all the details! On the other hand, there are people who want every possible detail about your offer. Make your headings summarize the whole story—this is for the impulse buyer. The details which follow these sub-headlines and paragraph headings are read by the detail-oriented person.

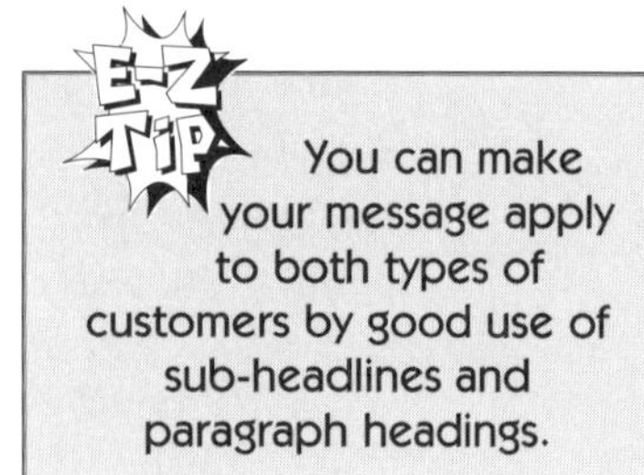

- ***Be specific:*** Specifics lend credibility to your claims. Rather than "I saved LWT, Inc. thousands of dollars in travel expenses since they began using our service," use "In the 87 days since LWT, Inc. started using our services, I slashed their travel expenses by $3,798.52!" See how much more believable the second sentence is? By the way, that kind of a claim would be even more believable if it was coming from someone at "LWT, Inc." (a testimonial).

- ***Talk in the first person:*** Don't promote yourself as a cold, non-person company. Write your material so that you are talking to the reader. Whatever you do, don't talk in the third person—detached from the

> *note*
>
> People like to know there is an INDIVIDUAL, a real PERSON who is taking RESPONSIBILITY for all the claims in the sales message.

person you're addressing. Don't say, "While examining your records, a preference for miniature doll furniture was observed. As a result, we are happy to present you with this special offer!" How cold and detached! Instead, say "I noticed you enjoy collecting miniature doll furniture, so I thought you would appreciate this special discount offer!" That's a much warmer message, wouldn't you agree?

KEYS TO SUCCESS

Test, test, test

Direct marketing is an iterative process. You do the best you can, and see what happens. Then you ever so slightly adjust your advertising message or methods, and try it again. Compare your results with the last time. Change something else, and try it again. It's very much like scientific experimentation because you always have a control group that you compare your "experimental group" against.

You want to test different headlines, different body copy, ordering coupons, colors, prices, advertising media, bonus offers—just about everything! When you test, always change only one thing at a time. Otherwise you don't know what's responsible for any differences you observe.

At times, you will be amazed at the big differences that can come about by very small changes!

As you read about copywriting techniques, you notice that not all the experts say the same thing. For instance, Ted Nicholas insists that short headlines are best—never more than 17 words. Contrast that to Dan Kennedy, who regularly uses much longer headlines. Both of these men are at the top of the direct marketing field, and both speak from many years of experience.

So what do you do? TEST. See what works for your offer. These men are experts, but they haven't sold your product or service. After you do some testing, you are the best judge of what works for your offer!

> **E-Z TIP** Test two different sales messages at the same time—just be sure you "code" the response mechanism (a code on your order form, for instance) so that you know which piece generated each order.

Don't become lazy about this. Once you start to taste some success, you'll be tempted to take it easy, cut some corners, ignore the boring, tedious parts of direct response marketing. Don't do it! No matter what anyone else says, I'm telling you that continued success requires continued work. Not hard work, not unpleasant work, but work. You must continue to take care of all the details—all the things that were responsible for making you a success in the first place. Or, you could just start over from the beginning. It's your choice.

Turning failure into success

If you know what I mean when I say "the money is in the back end" then you can skip this part.

You can become very wealthy even if your advertisements or sales letters lose money. The key is in using your leads and customer list effectively to generate *back-end* sales—sales that happen after the customer's initial purchase.

Here's an example. Suppose you mailed 5,000 letters to a list, and after all the orders came in, this is what you had:

No. of orders:	50 (1% response rate)
Profit per order:	$45 (after product and fulfillment costs)
Total income (50 X $45):	$2,250.00
Cost of mailing:	$2,500.00
Profit or loss:	<$250.00> LOSS

note

If the first product they bought from you met or exceeded their expectations, you can expect a good number of them to order from you again.

Oh no, you lost money, all your efforts have been in vain! Or have they? If you have a "back end" program—an assortment of other RELATED products you can sell to your customers, then you could mail another sales letter to those 50 customers shortly after they get their order from you. And, your back end offer can cost significantly higher than the front end. Let's see how this works out in dollars and cents:

No. of orders:	10 (20% of the 50 customers)	
Profit per order:	$90	
(your "back end" offer costs twice as much, and has double the profit)		
Total income (10 X $90):	$900.00	
Cost of mailing:	$ 25.00	
Profit or Loss:	$875.00 PROFIT	
Total Profit or Loss:	$875 - $250 =	$625 PROFIT

So, you turned what looked like a $250 loss into a $625 short term profit! The best part is that you can mail to these same customers over and over again—their "lifetime value" could be many hundreds or thousands of dollars each!

The same logic can be applied to a display ad that results in less sales volume than ad cost—as long as you generate customers, and if you have a good product and good back-end offers, you can still do great!

If you really want to do well, you must read more about it!

Remember, please remember, this is a very fundamental treatment of the concepts discussed—I only included this information because I thought it better to do so than to assume that my customers are familiar with it already. You need to understand at least the fundamentals in order to understand the later chapters of this guide.

Do yourself a favor, and purchase (or check out from your library) some of the books I recommended in the Resources/References Chapter. Don't kid yourself into thinking that the information you read thus far is all you'll ever need, because it's not! It is only the bare minimum of an education in copywriting and direct marketing, and we all (even the "gurus") need to participate in continual learning if we expect to be successful.

New tools for the small business owner

2

Chapter 2

New tools for the small business owner

What you'll find in this chapter:

- Fax, voice mail, and order-taking services
- Accepting credit cards
- Promotional items and incentives
- E-mail and your web site
- Discussion groups and search engines

If you kept up with technology, you will notice that some of the tools discussed here have actually been around for a little while—but they were too expensive for many small/home businesses to consider. Fortunately, these tools followed the rapid drop in prices for most electronic technologies.

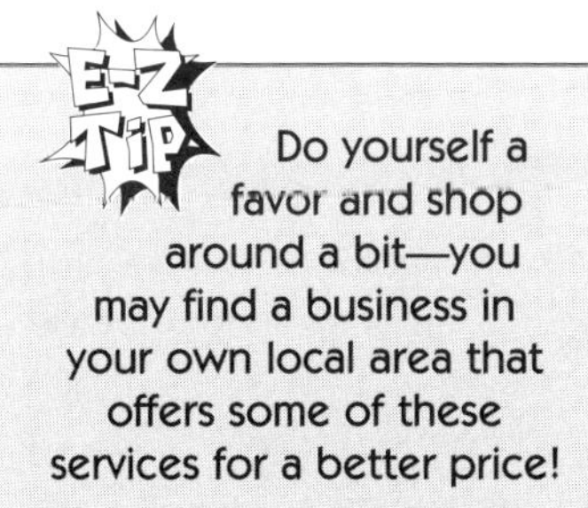

Do yourself a favor and shop around a bit—you may find a business in your own local area that offers some of these services for a better price!

With these new and affordable tools, you can compete on equal terms with the large companies. Indeed, you have some distinct advantages over these red-tape-filled and inefficient organizations!

As part of this discussion, I give you some information (contact information, prices, services offered, etc.) about various companies. While every effort was made to be accurate, you should always check with the companies yourself. Services offered and prices change. You can count on it! Also, none of my references to these companies constitute an endorsement or recommendation, nor a guarantee that theirs is the best or least expensive service.

You may find some of the discussion a bit too elementary for your level of experience, and for this I apologize. I thought it was best to assume no knowledge about the various marketing tools because you can always skip over the parts you already know.

NON-INTERNET-BASED MARKETING TOOLS

Fax

I suspect that everyone reading this guide is familiar with the facsimile (FAX) machine—they've been around for years. The problem many small/home businesses have, though, is keeping the FAX line open for faxes 24 hours a day. The FAX line is often shared with either a voice line or a computer modem line.

The ideal situation is to have one line used for voice, one used for data (the computer) and one for the FAX machine. However, adding a third line can be a real problem if your home/office is not wired for more than two lines.

There are several companies that receive and store faxes for you. This allows you to have a dedicated fax line without tying up your own phone line—so your customers never get a busy signal when they try to send you a fax, and you don't worry about whether you're missing one! Some services even page you or send you an e-mail when you receive a fax.

The fax service I use costs $15/month, regardless of the number of faxes I receive. They send me an e-mail whenever a fax is received, and I download the fax over the Internet. Though I don't use it, this company also offers voice mail services for an additional $5/month.

Fax-on-demand

Fax-on-demand is a service that allows your customers to request—and receive immediately—information about your company's products or services 24 hours a day, with no action on your part. Here's how it works:

The customer calls a number you gave them, and enters the number of the document they want. As an example, let's consider someone selling nutritional products. They might have the following documents listed in their literature:

0000	Index / List of all available Fax-on-Demand documents
1001	Information about our company and how our supplements are made
2000	Product Line Summary
2005	Stabilized Oxygen
2010	Anti-Oxidant combination
2015	Natural Mineral Supplement
2020	Enzyme Supplements
2025	Multi-vitamin Supplement
3000	Testimonials from our customers
4000	Order form

If you were the customer, and wanted information on vitamins, minerals, and enzymes, this is what you would do:

1) You call the fax-on-demand number from your fax machine—you would hear a message saying something like this:

   Thank you for calling ABC Nutrition's fax-on-demand system. In order to use this system, you must be calling from your FAX machine. You may select up to three documents during this call. Please select a document number followed by the pound sign.

2) You then type in (using your fax machine keypad) 2015# (minerals). The FOD (fax-on-demand) system would then reply:

   You selected document number two-zero-one-five. If you would like to get another document, please enter the document number followed by the pound sign. If you selected all the desired documents, just hit the pound sign by itself.

3) You then type in 2020# (enzymes)

   The FOD replies in the same was as in step #2

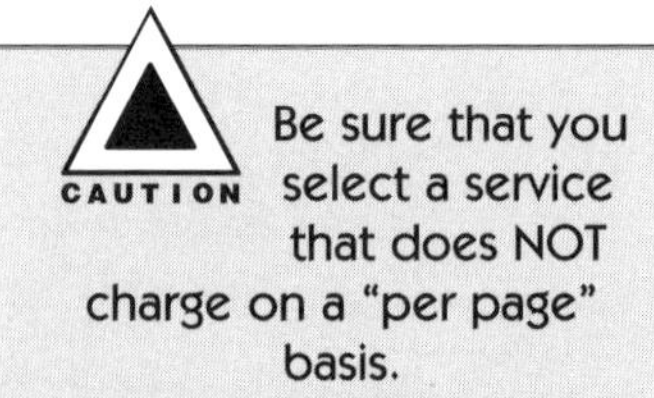

4) You then type in 2025# (vitamins)

   This time the FOD system says something like, *That was the last document for this call. Please hit the "Start" or "Send" button on your fax machine to receive the selected documents.*

5) You hit the Start/Send button on your fax machine, and the documents is sent to your fax machine immediately!

There are several companies that offer this service, but shop around for best price and service. You want a flat-rate monthly fee, and you don't want to be charged an exorbitant amount for every update or change you make. Two companies in the Resource Chapter offer fax-on-demand service for $5.00 per month!

Voice mail/transcription services

Answering machines have been around for a long time. But, in recent years, something a lot more powerful has become commonplace—voice mail. The biggest advantage of voice mail is that more than one person can leave a message for you at the same time. With an answering machine, if one person leaves a message, anyone else that calls gets a busy signal.

Likewise, if you use your phone at the time someone else calls you, that person gets your voice-mail service rather than a busy signal. For this to be true with your home or office voice line, you need to get the "call busy forwarding" service—check with your phone company and see if this is a service they offer. If your phone company doesn't offer this service, there are several other companies that do, and prices can be as low as $5/month!

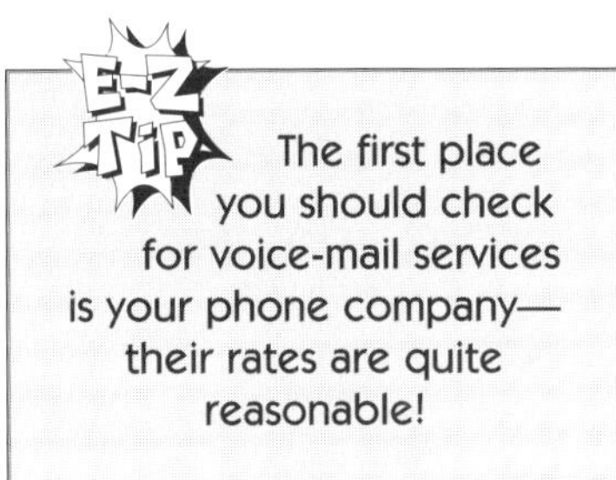

If you use voice mail for respondents of your classified or display advertising, you may find the "transcription" services of some companies to be of use as well. These companies set you up with a voice mail service, and when calls come in, they transcribe the name/phone/address information FOR YOU, and send that information to you via fax or e-mail. This is quite a time saver, and allows you to focus your efforts on more important tasks!

Tele-seminars

This is something that Joe Schroeder uses to great advantage. Take your basic voice mail service, make the outgoing message (the one your callers hear before leaving a message) 20-30 minutes long instead of 2-3, and end the call when the message is done playing—no attempt is made to record any information from the caller.

I know what you're thinking: "What use is that?!"

I'll use Joe Schroeder as an example—after all, I learned about this from him! Joe has a system that allows him to recruit large numbers of people into his MLM organization without the traditional one-on-one methods. He does this by stringing a bunch of tools together:

1) He advertises in a "business opportunity" or MLM-based publication. The ad refers to a 800 number for more information.

> note
>
> The tele-seminar is a tool that must be used in conjunction with other tools . . . e-mail, 1-800 number, fax-on-demand, etcetera.

2) The prospect calls the 800 number, is given a little pitch, and is referred to a FOD (fax on demand) for more information.

3) The fax on demand contains one or two (or more) tele-seminar numbers for the prospect to call.

4) The tele-seminars talk up the opportunity and refer the prospect back to the FOD, or to a different FOD, or to Joe's voice number.

That may seem like an awful lot of trouble to put the prospect through, but for Joe, that was the whole purpose. When someone finally worked through all of that and got Joe's number, he knew they were serious about the opportunity. Also, it was a system that the prospect could envision working for themselves—a way to sort and qualify prospects before you spend any time with them.

You might not want to put your prospects through everything that Joe does, but you could still use the tele-seminars to help sell the prospect on your product or service.

Interactive voice mail

Closely related to regular voice mail is interactive voice mail. In fact, I'm sure you "interacted" with voice mail already! Anytime you get a recording, "Press 1 for sales, 2 for customer service, 3 for technical support," you reached an interactive voice mail system.

There's a lot you can do with interactive voice mail. Besides directing your customers to different "departments," you can actually use the system to take orders. You can have the system set up like so:

1) Your customer calls and is greeted with *Thank you for calling ABC Nutrition's automatic ordering system! If you would prefer to talk to a real person, please dial (555) 555-5555 . Otherwise, please press the pound ('#') sign.*

2) Your customer presses the pound sign, and hears, *Which item or items would you like to order? Please speak clearly, and press the pound sign when you are finished.*

You can use an interactive voice mail system to make you look like a much larger company, if that's what you want.

3) Your customer lists the item(s) of interest, and presses the pound sign.

4) Your system replies *Thank you! Now I need to get your billing information. Please state your name and press the pound sign.*

5) Your customer states his name, and presses the pound sign. The system then proceeds to ask for the customer's billing address, phone number, and credit card number, or whatever information you require. Every piece of information is asked for and received in the same manner as the previous examples.

6) When finished gathering all the information, the systems says, *Thank you for your order! To send this order, press the "1" and then press the pound sign. To cancel, you may press the "star" key and hang up.*

There are some limitations to this system—and I wouldn't recommend its exclusive use for taking orders—because people are more comfortable talking to a real person when placing an order, especially when a credit card number is involved. However, this system could be used for the dissemination of other information, or as a temporary solution to your need for 24 hour order-taking until you can afford a "live" service.

Inbound order taking services

Most people have called a 1-800 order line at one time or another. There are many companies that contract out to take these calls and forward the ordering information on to you for processing and fulfillment.

Many (most?) of these companies are set up for large volume accounts with minimum monthly charges set at $150 or more. But, if you call around and explain your situation, you may find a company that works out a special "low volume" deal with you. I did this and found a company that takes orders for me 24 hours a day for $50/month + $0.69/minute. You may find better.

If not, no matter. There is a Canadian company that will give you this service—including an 800 number for your customers to call—for $30/month + $1.00/minute! Average calls (responding to an ad for a single item) are 2 minutes in length.

> **note** Look in your local "yellow pages" under "Telephone Answering Services" You'll find several companies listed—the Fort Lauderdale, FL yellow pages has five pages of such listings!

I recently got a tip via my e-mail about a company that takes orders for $20/month + $0.20 / minute. At that price, I doubt it's a toll-free order line, and I know that the caller is greeted first with a recording before the "live" operator comes on—but it's something to look at if your budget is really tight.

Accepting credit cards

This isn't a "tool" per se, but it's important enough to your success that I felt compelled to include it. One of the "rules" of direct marketing is to make it as easy as possible for people to purchase your product or service, and that's what credit cards are all about!

Accepting credit cards is especially important if you expect to sell anything via direct response methods. Your ability to accept credit cards lends credibility to your company, and gives your prospects a heightened sense of security when considering their purchase.

There are two ways you can accept credit cards. The first, most common (and least expensive) way is to get your own credit card *merchant account* at a bank. The second way is to *outsource* your order-taking operations.

The first thing you should do is visit the bank where you have your business account(s) and talk to them about getting a credit card merchant account. If you have a storefront business, or if the majority of your sales come from situations where you are with the customer (i.e. not mail order or phone sales), you have a good chance of getting an account this way.

If you get most of your orders over the phone or by mail, you may be turned down. That's okay; there are several companies that make a business of working with what the credit card industry considers high-risk businesses. Generally they require a site inspection (this is required by some of the credit card companies now), and you need to either purchase or lease your credit card processing equipment from them. Several of these companies are listed in the Resource chapter.

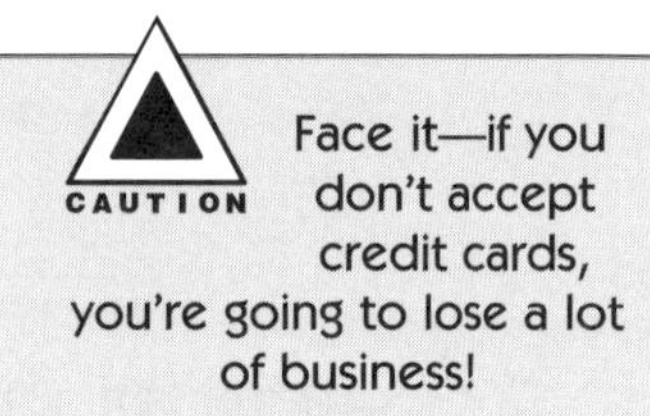

If for some reason you just CANNOT get a credit card merchant account, there are a couple of other options available. Several companies offer *outsourcing* for order processing, including credit card processing. They act as a commission dealer, selling your products or services and receiving a commission for the sales.

I found one company that does things a bit differently. They apply for a credit card merchant account on behalf of your business—the account has YOUR company name on it, but it is backed by the finances and reputation of this third party company, and all transactions go through them. This is an added level of security for the banks and for your customers.

In both of the above plans, you generally must wait a minimum of two weeks from when the orders are placed before you receive your money. Also, the cost of processing credit cards is higher this way . . . but it beats not taking credit cards at all!

Checks by fax or phone

Though not as important as the ability to accept credit cards, the ability to accept checks by fax or phone can add considerably to your bottom line. It is especially useful if you want to accept orders by fax and the customer doesn't have a major credit card. There are two methods for accepting fax checks:

- **Software:** You can purchase "Fax Check" software that allows you to input all the required information (as given to you by your customer) and then print a check, which you can deposit in your account. The check does not require a signature. The highest price I saw for this software is $349.00 and the lowest I saw is $25.00 (see the Resource chapter). Don't worry, this really works. I deposited many checks that were generated in this way!

- **Services:** If you don't have a computer or don't want to do it yourself, there are companies that process the fax/phone checks for you. You just send them the information and they create the check for you. The cost for this service is about $1.00 per check in low volume, sometimes less if you have more checks.

Travel incentives and other promotional items

Have you ever seen one of those car dealership advertisements offering "A Free 3 day/2 night Bahamas Vacation With Every Test Drive?" How are they able to pay for all those free vacations and still make money on the cars they sell? I know, I know, you're thinking something about those slick car salespeople and what the car REALLY costs them in the first place! Bad example on my part, I suppose . . . but seriously, how can companies pay for free vacations for people who don't even buy their product?

The answer is: They don't pay very much for the vacation packages. If five people test drive a car, and only one buys, the dealer pays for the five vacation packages and still makes a profit. I would love to tell you exactly how little these vacation packages cost, but for legal reasons I can't.

However, I have listed a few companies in the References/Resources Chapter that sell these packages. Because they have other distributors that sell these same packages at different prices, I can't publish their prices—just contact them directly and find out for yourself, you'll be amazed!

> **E-Z TIP** Depending on your what your main product or service is, you may be able to offer on-phone consulting time as a bonus when people make a purchase, or perhaps a newsletter subscription.

Besides travel packages, there are many other promotional items you can give away to spice up your offers. One of the best (and lowest cost) items you can offer is an "information product" related to your product or service. These can have very high perceived value and can be created for next to nothing!

Of course, there are the conventional items too—pens, refrigerator magnets, mugs—all imprinted with your sales message and contact information. Some sources for these kind of products are listed in the Reference/Resource Chapter.

INTERNET-BASED MARKETING TOOLS

If you are not yet on the Internet, I urge you to start learning about it. The best way to do this is to subscribe to an online service and start looking around—start experimenting—now! Many of the newest and most cost effective business tools are only available on the Internet, and you do yourself a great disservice by not taking advantage of them. Don't be afraid of the Internet—it is a powerful tool that you SHOULD be using to help build your business.

You may find it helpful to enlist the help of a friend or acquaintance when you first start. People are usually very happy to share their Internet tips and tricks with anyone who asks! If you don't know anyone who is on the Internet, contact your local high school or adult education program, and see if they can recommend a student or class to help you get started. The cost will be minimal, and the time they save you will be more than worth it! If this isn't a comfortable scenario for you, there are many books about the Internet for beginners—buy one or check one out from the library, and get started—now!

Like anything else, developing a proficiency with Internet technology requires time. If you don't have time, there are always people who will be willing to set up your site for a fee—and perhaps it is worth it to you to pay someone rather than do any of the work on your own—if you are in a position to do that, more power to you! Just show your Internet consultant the tools discussed in this guide and let them make the arrangements!

Before I start explaining the various Internet-based marketing tools, there are some terms that must be defined. You Internet-savvy people can skip this part if you want.

What is the Internet?

Consider a company that has 50 employees at their head office, each with a computer at their desk. Connecting these computers together to form a network allows the employees to:

- send messages to each other through their computers
- access others' computer files
- share printers or other external resources (e.g., the printer might be physically connected to Mary's computer, but everyone in the company could send documents to that printer over the network)

The computers are connected with special networking hardware, usually a networking interface card and a cable. If I unplug the cable, then I have no access to the network resources (files, printers, etc.). I would be limited to working with files residing on my own computer, and with devices connected directly to it. This is often referred to as a *Local Area Network (LAN)*.

Suppose this same company had sales offices in different parts of the world, each office with its own LAN system. Using the telephone system and/or satellite links, the company could connect all the LANs together, thus creating a *Wide Area Network (WAN)*, sometimes referred to as an *Intranet*. The "Intra-" denotes that the network is all within the same company—no one from outside the company can access any of the files or other resources connected to this company's intranet. The company can, however, make portions of their network accessible by outside parties, if they so choose.

That brings us to the definition of the Internet:

The *Internet* is simply a worldwide network of computers. While many companies have computers that are connected to the Internet full-time, most individuals connect their computer to the Internet for only brief periods of time (through their phone line). They log on to the system, stay connected for a period of time, and then log off the system again. This is referred to as a *dial-up connection.*

Once your computer is connected to the Internet, you can send messages to other computers (actually to the people operating the computers) that are also on the Internet. You can also access billions of files on computer systems throughout the world!

I'm sure many consider the above an oversimplified definition of the Internet, but for our purposes, it tells everything we need to know. Don't get carried away with all the hyperbole about the Internet. Think of it as a communications and research tool, for that is exactly what it is . . . no more, no less! What makes it so powerful is the speed with which these communications take place, and the extremely low cost when compared with other methods.

What is E-mail?

Electronic mail or *E-mail* is a way to send messages to other people through a computer network. In most cases, e-mail is sent through the use of an e-mail program. There are several free e-mail programs available, check the Resource Chapter for details. Anyone who has an Internet presence has e-mail at the very minimum. People send e-mail to your e-mail address, which are something like this: **paulg@palis.com** (that's my actual e-mail address).

DEFINITION

You might be interested to know that there is at least one e-mail program that you can use to send e-mail to people without having an Internet account. You can send and receive e-mail completely free of cost! You DO need at the very minimum, a computer with a *modem*—this is a device allows the computer to communicate with other computers via your phone line.

> *note*
>
> A modem comes standard on most computers today, and can be purchased for less than $50 if you don't have one already.

You may be wondering, "How can I receive e-mail if my computer is not connected to the Internet full time? If Aunt Monica sends me an e-mail at 2 p.m., and I don't log on (check my e-mail) until 4 p.m., what happens to the e-mail?!" Relax, you won't miss any of your e-mail. When your Aunt Monica sends you e-mail, it is temporarily stored on your e-mail service provider's computer until you log on and download it to your own computer.

What is the World Wide Web?

Some people think that the Internet and the world wide web are the same thing, but they're not. The World Wide Web (often shortened to just "Web" or "WWW") is a part of the Internet, but there are many computers on the Internet that are not part of the world wide web. Documents on the WWW usually are formatted in the *Hypertext Markup Language (HTML),* which supports links to other documents, pictures, sound files, even video. These are all considered resources on the world wide web. Simply clicking on these links load the referenced resource.

All resources on the WWW have their own unique "address," similar to the following:

http://www.palis.com/index.htm
(that's the address of my own web site, by the way)

To access WWW resources, you must have a *browser* program. The two most common browsers are Netscape and Microsoft Internet Explorer. There are other browsers, but I recommend sticking with one of these two—they are as close to a standard as is available so far. Usually when you sign up for an Internet account you receive browser software as part of the service.

A web site is just a collection of pages/documents/files owned and managed by the same company or individual. Each document has links to other documents. These links can be to documents at other web sites as well as to other documents on your own web site. And, documents can be text, pictures, animations, sound clips, video—just about anything! You can have your own web site, free of charge—just keep reading to find out how (or skip to the Resources Chapter).

SIG files

DEFINITION

In many Internet forums, advertising is frowned upon. However, at the end of your message, you are always allowed to include a brief statement about yourself, your company, your web site, whatever. This is called a *signature file* or *SIG file* for short. Most e-mail programs can be configured to include the SIG file automatically on all your outgoing e-mails, and some newsgroup readers can do the same.

In the beginning, it wasn't acceptable to have a SIG file longer than four lines, but as the Internet has become more commercialized, longer SIG files have become common. Use common sense, don't abuse your privileges, and model your SIG file after others in your particular forum.

Here is an example SIG file (this is one I use):

```
Paul Galloway
--------------------------------------------------------------------------
        * DIRECT MARKETING * MLM * INTERNET MARKETING *
     FREE Access to 1300+ Business and Consumer-Related Reports
             ALL ONLINE FOR YOUR IMMEDIATE USE!
                    http://www.palis.com
--------------------------------------------------------------------------
```

Tools to use

Okay, now that wee covered the definitions, let's jump right into some of the new tools available to small/home business owners.

E-mail

Yes, yes, I know I discussed e-mail earlier, but that was just a definition—now I'm talking about the TOOL. As Internet tools go, e-mail was one of the first—and it is still the most useful tool of all. E-mail was referred to many times as the "killer application" for marketing on the Internet. The reason is that it is the most widely available Internet-based communications tool.

There are many people who DO have e-mail, but do not yet have access to the WWW. Some businesses make the mistake of including their WWW address on their literature, but not their e-mail address—effectively barring those people who only have e-mail from doing business with them! Don't make this mistake.

E-mail is fast. Most of the e-mail I send is received within a couple of minutes. One of the goals of your other Internet (and conventional!) marketing should be to capture the e-mail addresses of your customers and prospects. You can follow up quickly and inexpensively (can you say "free"), and much of the process can be automated.

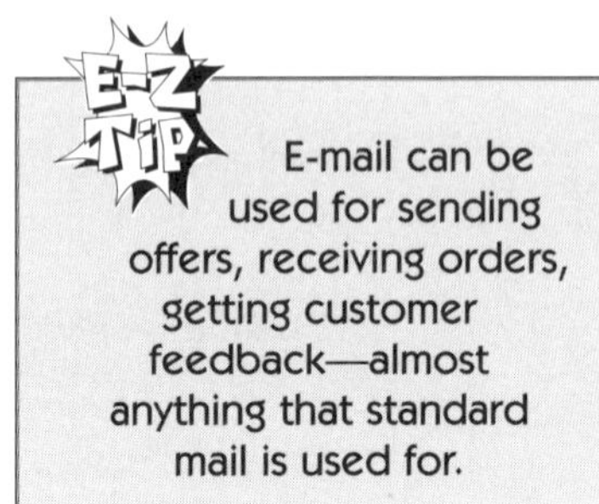

E-mail can be used for sending offers, receiving orders, getting customer feedback—almost anything that standard mail is used for.

Bulk e-mail (don't do it!)

I only mention bulk e-mail here because I want to warn you against using it. First of all, what is bulk e-mail? *Bulk e-mail* is the practice of sending out thousands of e-mails to people who have never heard of you or your company, and have NOT requested you to send them anything.

Not only would I advise you to not do this, but I would even go so far as to recommend that you *don't send any quantity of unsolicited e-mail.* There are other ways to get customers without putting your online resources at risk. That's right, if you send out unsolicited e-mails, you risk losing your Internet access! Public and government sentiment is very much against this right now (even though junk conventional mail is okay—go figure), so at the very least you'll give yourself a bad reputation.

Recently this message was posted to an online discussion group. Pay attention to what this person says:

> Don't Drink - It will ruin your liver
> Don't Smoke - It will give you lung cancer
> Don't Walk in Front of a Bus - You will be squashed
>
> Well, now there's a new one to add to the list......

DON'T BULK E-MAIL..... That's Right.....

DON'T BULK E-MAIL..... I'll say it once more for the dummies....

DON'T BULK E-MAIL.....

It is the most certain way to cause you death in cyberspace.

Perhaps I should explain exactly what I am talking about.

I run a Direct Marketing Company. Not a large one, there's only me.

What they all say is true. It's the perfect lifestyle, the profits are terrific, and If I don't feel like working today, I just switch the business into auto mode.

I've been in operation now for around 3 months, 2 of those was setting up the business. I opened my doors in the traditional way, mail outs,fax outs, classified ads. These worked well. However, there was one part of my business which needed a boost (so to speak), the Website.

I'd heard it all before. What ever you do - DON'T BULK E-MAIL. I subscribe to a number of newsletters, have spent over $10,000 on direct marketing material to find out from the greats how to promote yourself, and they ALL say the SAME THING - DON'T BULK E-MAIL.

Why didn't I listen to them. I'd paid out all this money for the best information, yet I completely ignored it.

I'd got one of those e-mailing programs, and it just so happened that I had half a million e-mail addresses lying around.

My intentions were to test out the program so that I could use it with my own database that I had gathered. So I did. 2000 names to be exact. That's right —I only tested out 2,000 names.

I went away from the computer and made myself a milkshake. I was happy. I had just sent 2000 people a mailing which would normally take a day to do using conventional methods, and it had hardly cost me anything.

BIG MISTAKE!!!

I had heard of the affectionate term of spamming before, so when I came back to my computer, I checked my e-mail - Terrific, only 30 people had sent the message back to me. I disconnected my modem and did some other work. I went to hook back onto the Internet 15 minutes later, and it came up with this message.....

USER UNKNOWN..... I must have typed in the wrong password.

USER UNKNOWN..... Gee's, twice in a row.

USER UNKNOWN...... What's going on here..

It was funny, even though I had only sent 2,000 names, I had this strange feeling that my ISP had blocked my account. I didn't believe it of course, I had only sent 2,000 e-mails, and this is a big ISP (Telstra—Our main phone carrier in Australia). I had just spent $200 on one of those new 56k modems the day before (this is the only ISP in Australia which has 56k access).

I rang up their FREECALL number and after being on hold for 15 minutes, All I could be told was that someone had closed the account.

"WHAT DO YOU MEAN, SOMEONE HAS CLOSED THE ACCOUNT??????"

"Well Sir, the account was closed because a number of messages were spammed to you Sir."

"SO THAT'S IT? THE ACCOUNT IS CLOSED, AND THERE'S NOTHING I CAN DO ABOUT IT?"

"You may appeal the decision by writing to this address."

Get this, a SERVICE PROVIDER closed my account on the spot and told me that I may APPEAL THE DECISION!!!

It doesn't sound too much like a service to me.

What all the above amounts to is this:

1) I cannot access my e-mail. That's right, orders, leads etc.....
2) I can't even hook onto the Internet
3) All my stationery now has the wrong address on it.
4) Anyone who I have given my address to, will be sending their e-mail to the dead e-mail letter office.

CAUTION

There are some people that maintain they have every right to send e-mail to anyone, anytime, for any reason—and from a legal standpoint they may be right (at least at the time of publication). However, given the public attitude about it, I recommend you NOT do it!

"Opt-in" direct E-mail

You'll get your best response from e-mail solicitations sent to past customers or people who asked you for more information—just like with conventional mail. However, sometimes you may want to send targeted e-mail to people you never interacted with before. As discussed previously, bulk e-mail is NOT the recommended way of doing this . . . but *opt in* e-mail is!

Opt-in e-mail lists are made up of people who have specifically requested information from advertisers like you. There are some companies that sell e-mail lists of people with specific interests who said "Yes, please distribute my name to advertisers—I WANT to hear what people offer in this (specific) area of interest!" Well, there you go, sounds like a pretty good prospect to me. These names aren't cheap—they cost 10 to 25 cents EACH, but hey, compare that to the cost of sending conventional mail to them. In fact, let's DO the comparison for a test mailing of 1,000 people:

	Conventional Mail	Direct E-mail
Average Cost of Targeted List	$75.00	$150.00
Average Cost of Sales Materials	$200.00	$0.00
Cost of Mailing	$320.00	$0.00
TOTAL	$595.00	$150.00

Some people argue that this comparison isn't fair because I'm using first class postage rates. Well, there are several experts who say that is the ONLY way to send out direct mail, and that is what I do myself (more about that in Chapter Three). Even with third class postage, the total would still be about three times as high as the cost of doing a direct e-mail.

One more e-mail advantage to consider is the number of people who will actually READ your message—a much higher percentage read the e-mail. At the very LEAST they read the headline (subject line of the e-mail) which is more than you could hope for in your wildest direct (conventional) mail dreams!

One more"secret." There's one opt-in e-mail broker I know of who gives you a chance to earn credits you can redeem for the purchase of targeted e-mail lists. For every person I send to this company (via their banner ad on my web site)—and who signs up for one of their opt-in lists—I get to mail to 15 people from whichever target list I choose, with an average value of $2.25 for each sign-up!

Check out the Resource Chapter for more information on this and other direct e-mail companies.

List servers

A *list server* is something like an automated mailing list manager for your e-mail addresses. Once you set it up it will:

1) Automatically process requests by your prospects to be placed on your mailing list

2) Automatically process requests to be REMOVED from your mailing list

3) Mail your message to everyone on the mailing list. You send the message to your list server, and it sends that message to everyone on your list, with no more work from you!

4) Automatically remove "bounced" e-mail addresses from your mailing list

Simply put, a list server relieves you from all the tedium of list management. Your customers and prospects are able to automatically subscribe or unsubscribe to your mailing list (newsletter, bulletin, electronic magazine or "e-zine"), rather than bothering you with the task. When you want to send a message to everyone on your list, you send a single e-mail to your list server and it sends copies of that e-mail to everyone on your distribution list.

As I mentioned, you should make every attempt in your marketing efforts to capture the e-mail addresses of your customers and prospects. If you e-mail them often (and you should), a list server saves you untold hours of work.

E-Z TIP: Once you DO send out an e-mail, if some of the e-mail addresses are no longer valid (causing an e-mail "bounce"), those addresses will be removed (automatically) from your list!

Actually, the list server's original intended purpose is for anyone on the subscriber list to be able to send a single e-mail to the list server, and then have the list server redistribute that e-mail to everyone else on the list. You could use it in this manner as well, if you wanted—it would be an "e-mail discussion group" in that case, and that might be a good thing to offer your customers.

The best known commercial list server programs are *Majordomo* and *Listserv*. These were designed for heavy commercial use. They are very feature rich and robust, and their cost reflects this—they are licensed on a yearly basis, and the license fee includes support, should you need it. Most small/home businesses simply cannot afford these packages—and even if they could, most don't have the necessary computer resources or technical expertise to run them.

CAUTION: There are some ISPs that simply won't allow a list server—they'll be too afraid of the problems that could come up if your list traffic grows too large.

The freeware alternative is *Minordomo* (don't you just love how computer people play with words?)—it can be set up on your existing

Internet account IF your Internet Service Provider (ISP) allows you to do so. It requires a little setup, but nothing your competent Internet Consultant can't handle. Still, in my opinion, there are even better alternatives for the home/small business owner.

The first thing you should do is ASK your ISP if they offer list server services—many do, and for a small increase in your monthly Internet service fee, they host your list. They take care of all the technical aspects—all you need to know is the e-mail address to send your messages to. Well, actually, there are a couple other things you'll probably want to know, like how to manually add/delete names from your e-mail list, but the point is you have a much simpler time if your ISP is hosting the list for you.

There are also some companies that offer to host your list server on their own system—for a monthly fee. The fees I've seen range from $9.95/month up to $100/month or more, depending on how heavily the list server is used. See the Resource Chapter for details about getting your own list server service.

Besides having your own e-mail list, you should check out any e-mail lists run by others who share your business interests. Sometimes they are promoted as e-zines (electronic magazines) or newsletters, but they work the same way as the e-mail lists I discussed in this chapter.

Not only can they be invaluable for research, many of them offer classified advertising, and usually their advertising rates are much lower than the corresponding rates found in conventional media.

There are over 84,000 of these e-mail lists. Some allow subscribers to send messages to everyone on the list (*read/write lists*), and others are *read only lists*—run like a newsletter or bulletin—where only the list owner is allowed to send out messages to the subscribers. While the read/write lists are the most valuable (allowing you to interact with the other list members) from a research and feedback standpoint, the read only lists can help you learn more about the other people/companies in your field. All the newsletters and e-zines that allow classified advertising are read only lists, and this makes them extremely valuable from a marketing perspective.

Remember to NOT advertise on any of the read/write e-mail lists—you'll be banned from the list, and get a bad reputation among the people whose trust and cooperation you most need. Your SIG file is allowable, as long as it's not too many lines in length and is not too loud.

Along with the list serve information in the Resources Chapter, I listed some e-mail list references for you to check out. Sign up for a few and see how they run. Have fun!

Autoresponders

An *autoresponder* is the Internct e-mail equivalent of a fax-on-demand system. It has also been called an *E-mail on Demand System, E-mail Robot, Mailbot* or *Automated E-mail.* Just like a FOD system, an autoresponder is designed to immediately disseminate information to whomever asks for it, whenever they ask for it, with no action required by you. As such, I consider it one of the most powerful of all the tools discussed in this guide.

There are several ways an autoresponder can be set up. One way is to have an e-mail address assigned to a separate autoresponder for each document you want to make available. Whenever someone sends an e-mail to that address, the receiving computer automatically—and immediately—sends an e-mail reply to the sender. The reply would contain whatever document you assigned to that particular autoresponder when you set it up.

note

Note that it doesn't matter what the prospect says in the subject field or body of the e-mail—everything is ignored by the receiving computer except the sender's return e-mail address.

With this setup, you need a different autoresponder address for every document you want to make available. This could be considered a disadvantage, but there are some definite advantages to this system too, as you will see.

Another way of setting up an autoresponder is to have a single address for an unlimited number of documents. However, with this method, the computer evaluates the text in the subject or body of the "request" e-mail. For instance, suppose your company had three documents—document #1, document #2, and document #3—for distribution via autoresponder.

E-Z TIP

The "one e-mail address for each document" method is probably the choice for your prospect, and much more "foolproof" than other systems.

Your prospects are given the instructions to send an e-mail to "autosend@abcnutrition.com" (or whatever your autoresponder's e-mail address is), and they are also told to type the words "get document #1" in the body of the e-mail. Or, with some autoresponder systems, they need to type "document #1" in the subject of the e-mail.

This method has the advantage of requiring only one e-mail address no matter how many documents you want to make available to your prospects.

However, it requires more work on the part of your prospect—and it allows more opportunity for error—some people might type the required information in the body of the e-mail instead of the subject field, or vice-versa. Other people might type "Please send me information about your nutrition supplements," and the computer would send them an error message.

A third method requires the use of a web page. The prospect is given a list of available documents and would click on or check the box in front of each document they desire. They then enter their e-mail address in the "Your E-mail Address" box. Finally, they click on the "Send Request" button.

I suppose this is the most foolproof of all the methods, as long as the prospect gives their proper e-mail address, but I don't really like this method for two reasons.

1) The prospect is reading a WWW page. If they want more information (like that contained in document #1), all you have to do is place that document on your web site and create a "link" to it. With this ability, it just doesn't make much sense to me to make them request the document and retrieve it via their e-mail program—which most likely is a separate program than the one they use to access the web.

2) This autoresponder is useless for people who have e-mail but don't have WWW access. Though the WWW is catching on quickly, there are many people who don't yet have access to it—but who DO have e-mail. That is one reason e-mail is still considered the best application for the Internet—everyone can use it.

Newsgroups

Newsgroups have been around for many years, yet I would venture a guess that a significant percentage of people on the Internet don't know what they are. Basically, a *newsgroup* is a message forum for people with a specific interest. There are newsgroups for just about anything anyone wants to talk about. In fact, there are over 30,000 different special-interest newsgroups. Business, religion, personal relationships, investing, items for sale, everything imaginable.

Don't just start posting advertisements to newsgroups. You could get in as much trouble as you would sending unsolicited bulk e-mail.

When you "post" a message to the newsgroup, everyone that has an interest in that subject can read your message, and can reply to it on the newsgroup or via e-mail (if you supply your e-mail address). Like e-mail and the WWW, you need specific software to read and post newsgroup messages—they are called "news readers," and they are usually included with your web browsing software (Netscape and Internet Explorer both have integrated newsreaders).

The reason newsgroups can be so valuable to the marketer is because they are already broken up into target markets—the name of the newsgroup defines the interests of the people participating in it. No matter what industry you deal with, you're sure to find at least one (if not several) newsgroup which appeals to your target market.

Make sure that any messages you post are relevant to the interest of the newsgroup—off topic posts will get you in trouble.

Be careful about posting ads to newsgroups—just like unsolicited e-mail, there are certain public attitudes about how newsgroups should be used.

They are intended to be forums for discussion, not advertising. The best use of news groups is for market research. Use these forums to gather information about your target market. The best way to do this is to participate in the discussions. One thing you can do, and which can be very effective, is to promote your business in these groups is to include your SIG file at the end of all your messages.

There are a few newsgroups where blatant advertising seems to go unpunished, and these are listed in the Reference Chapter. Their scope is limited, and they have a tendency to get clogged with a lot of junk—so don't get your hopes up.

Discussion groups

Also referred to as bulletin boards, discussion groups are very similar in function to newsgroups, but there are some important differences. The first (and major) difference, is that discussion groups are more local in nature.

Definition:

A *discussion group* is more like a big bulletin board set up in your home or store (or web page, in this case).

Try to think of a newsgroup as a global, electronic classified advertisements newspaper. No one is required to go to your store, they just read the messages under the category of interest. If they want, they can reply to the messages they see there by posting their own classified ad. Or, if they want to, they reply privately by whatever contact information is given in the message of interest. The point is, they never come to your place to read and/or reply to messages.

Now, contrast that to your discussion group. People can come to your location and post notes on the bulletin board. Other people who visit can read those notes, and can do one (or more) of three things:

1) post a reply (on the bulletin board) to the messages they read for all to see and reply to

2) use the contact information given by the note's author (phone, address, e-mail), and reply to that person privately (not on the bulletin board)

3) post their own note about something unrelated to any they read

But, they have to come to your web page to read or post messages. What a great way of getting people to come back to your site over and over again. Just let people know you are hosting a discussion group about whatever your business is. The more people that get involved, the more interesting it will be for everyone.

The best part is the software for running your own discussion group is absolutely free. Check the Resource Chapter for details!

note

If people are going to look for YOU or your product/service on the Internet, they will be looking for your web site, NOT your e-mail address (of course, your e-mail address will be listed on your web site).

Web sites

Web sites are the most popular of all Internet-based tools. Have you noticed a proliferation of the prefix "www?" United Parcel Service has "www.ups.com" on the side of all their delivery trucks. Magazines have their own web site www address, news stations (television) throw their WWW address on the screen at the end of news broadcasts—some even take polls via the web. The world wide web (of which all web pages are a part) is growing faster than any other facet of the Internet.

E-Z TIP

Give people a good reason for coming back to your site, because otherwise it is far too easy for them to leave and never come back.

Think of a web site as your own online store consisting of one or more web pages. It has its own unique address, and you can use it to showcase your products and/or services in various ways. You can use words, pictures, sound, animation, and video.

Don't use your web site like a billboard—unchanging and boring. Your web site can contain billboards (called Banner Advertisements), but they are a lot more than that. Just like a retail storefront, you must make an effort to change things frequently, give it a new look, add products or services, interact with the prospects in some way (drawing, survey, free samples, etcetera).

Your web site may have many functions, including:

- product research
- marketing research
- generation prospect leads
- customer support and feedback
- online sales (placed directly through your web site)

Let's briefly discuss each one of these:

Product research

E-Z TIP

Much of the power of the Internet is in the ability you have to interact with people quickly and easily. If you are developing a product, you can use your web site to solicit input from your target market. You can get suggestions for new products related to the ones you already sell. You can set up a discussion group for buyers of that product, and find out what your customers consider to be its strengths and weaknesses.

Marketing research

This overlaps product research in some respects—the feedback you receive about your products can help drive new marketing strategies. For instance, if you had previous customers fill out a survey about your product, you might see a pattern in the demographics. You might find that 80% of your customers were middle-income men, age 40-45. You might also find that 60% of your customers enjoyed reading *Mother Earth News*.

This information is invaluable when planning you next magazine display advertisement campaign, wouldn't you agree? You wouldn't use just customers for your marketing research, you could also use any visitors to your site—offer them something free just for filling out a short survey. If they come to your site and stay for more than 5 seconds, it's because they had at least a passing interest in whatever it is you offer. Find out what kind of people are interested in your site, and find out what other things they have in common.

Another way you can use your site is to test different advertising copy. Say you were doing a direct e-mail campaign, you could direct half your prospects to one sales message, and direct the other half to a slightly different message. Determining which message is better is a simple exercise of counting orders generated from each one.

Generation of prospect leads

On my site, I offer people the opportunity to access over 1,300 reports free of charge (most are about making or saving money, but there are some other general interest reports as well). But, there's a catch. They have to give me their e-mail address first. Of course you know why—so I can put them on my own "opt-in" e-mail list! Instead of offering free reports, you might opt to offer a "Tip of the Week" service to anyone that wants it, via e-mail. Some other people use their web sites to generate phone inquiries, or even to get prospects to come into a showroom and check out the latest model cars. It only takes one car sale to recoup the annual cost of a web site. Come to think of it, since you can actually get some web sites totally FREE, it wouldn't necessarily even take that.

Customer support and feedback

Besides the feedback mentioned in relation to product/marketing research, you could use your website to disseminate information to your customers upon request 24 hours a day. You could set up your own support discussion group; you might find that many of the questions your customers had are answered by other customers who had the same problem but found out how to solve it. When this happens, take note, and update your product documentation.

> note
>
> Several computer and electronics companies have their technical support libraries loaded onto a web site—at an annual savings of thousands (or millions!) of dollars when compared to previous methods.

Online sales

Last, but *certainly* not least, sales are your main goal. Some people use their web site to get online sales exclusively, but I recommend giving people other options as well. Some people just aren't comfortable entering their personal and credit card information at the computer. Though people can order online through my web site, they are also given the options of ordering by mail, FAX, or phone (voice)—and all of these methods are chosen by my customers. Who knows how many sales I would miss without offering a variety of ordering options?

Custom forms and scripts

DEFINITION

Forms are feedback pages on a web site, and *scripts* are the simple programs that intercept incoming form data and act on it. Compare this to the feedback cards at your local restaurant: A customer fills out the form and drops it in a box (or mails it to you). The restaurant manager reads this form, and may take several different actions. The difference is that in the restaurant example, everything occurs over a period of a few days or longer, while using forms on the Internet can allow the same things to happen in a matter of hours, minutes—even seconds! An example form I use on my own web site is shown on the next page:

Just fill out the form below and hit the submit button! You'll immediately be given the instructions for accessing more than 1200 business building and consumer-related reports. By the way. . .

Anyone who supplies their snail-mail address will receive our quarterly business resource catalog!

(Required Information)

NAME:
EMAIL:

(All information requested below is OPTIONAL)

Please tell us what kind of information you are most interested in obtaining here (you may check more than one!):

- ❒ Profitable Marketing of Your Products and Services
- ❒ Successful Consulting
- ❒ Making Money on the INTERNET
- ❒ General Business How-To Information
- ❒ Service Business How-To Information
- ❒ Personal Legal Kits & Software
- ❒ Successful Promotion of the MLM company you're already involved with
- ❒ A New MLM Opportunity which will pay $889/month with 20 people

If you want a free business resource catalog, fill in your "snail-mail" address below:

Address
Suite/Apt:
City:
State/Province:
Zip / Postal Code:
Country:

Do you have any comments for us? Anything you'd like to see here? Anything you'd like to gripe about? We welcome your comments!

Type your message here . . .

(Click on the below button to get your username/password!)

SEND ME THE USERNAME and PASSWORD FOR THE FREE REPORTS!

I believe that the majority of my online (Internet) sales come as a result of this form and the script that handles it.

This form is used to get information from prospects that visit my site. They are only required to submit their name and e-mail address, but many people go ahead and fill in the "snail mail" address. Many more check at least one of the interest boxes, which is great feedback for me when I evaluate how my site measures up to their needs.

Here's the best part though. Using a script, I automatically send an e-mail message about my MLM-related products to anyone who checks the MLM box. The prospect indicates their particular interest, and BOOM, they get a message from me showing how I can help them in that area. You can do the same.

> **E-Z TIP** Many basic forms and scripts are available free, and they can be easily modified to fit your own specific needs.

Most of the Web site creation tools (see the Resource Chapter for details) allow you to easily create a form, and there are free scripts available that process the form data once it is sent. The resource chapter also has the locations where you can download these free scripts.

Once you have the free scripts, you can usually modify them to suit your particular needs. Be sure to check the copyright information that comes with the script to be sure that the author has given you the right to modify their code. Any competent professional (or moderately experienced amateur) should be able to modify your scripts to your specific requirements in a surprisingly brief period of time (minutes to days, depending on your needs).

Perhaps the most important form you can have on your web site is the order form. Your customer types in the required information and clicks on the "Send Order" button, and voila, you have an order sitting in your e-mail box. Some Web ordering systems" even verify the credit card information while the customer stands by for the verification number.

Banners and exchanges

Here is the first Internet Banner Ad that I used:

FREE!!	Over 1300 Business AND Consumer-Related Reports That You Can Read ONLINE. Right NOW!

When this ad is seen on the WWW, people can click their mouse on it to go directly to my web site. Banner ads don't need to be as small as this one, they can be all different sizes, shapes, and colors. Now, there are even animated banners, which change from one image to the next, cause parts of the picture to flash, make words move across the banner—all kinds of nifty things.

I know what you're thinking, "Yeah, pretty nifty, but so what—how's it going to help ME?"

DEFINITION

It's true that this alone isn't all that exciting . . . but, I haven't told you everything yet! There are several companies that broker the exchange of banners—these are called *link exchanges*, and generally they work like this:

1) You sign up and place special HTML code on your web site (don't worry, it's simple, and the exchange gives you step by step instructions). This code causes a different banner ad to be displayed each time someone views your web page. The banner might be by the exchange themselves, or by someone else who is participating in the exchange just like you.

2) Every time the page containing that link is loaded, you get one "point." This doesn't mean that someone must click on that link, they just have to see it (which happens when they view your web page).

3) For every 2 "points," the exchange will see that YOUR banner ad is viewed on someone else's web page.

4) You can change your banner ad anytime you want.

Now, here's the best part.

Many link exchanges keep track of your statistics. You can pull up a web page that shows how many people saw your banner, and how many of those people actually clicked on it. Don't expect exceptional numbers here . . . the average (as far as I heard) is 100 to 150 viewings of your banner for every *click thru* (when someone sees your banner and clicks on it). Some people achieve click-thru ratios better than 10:1, which is 10-15 times better than the average—but they are being kind-of tricky. I'll show you in a minute what they are doing.

The point is this: you can use the banner exchanges to **TEST YOUR HEADLINES!** That's right. As an example, consider the banner ad I showed you above. After the banner ad ran little while, I checked the statistics page for the link exchange company I used, and found that 2,100 people saw the banner on various pages on the internet. Of those 2,100 people, a grand total of 10 people clicked on the banner to go to my page. That meant that in order to get one person to come to my site, 210 people need to see that particular banner ad—210. That's awful.

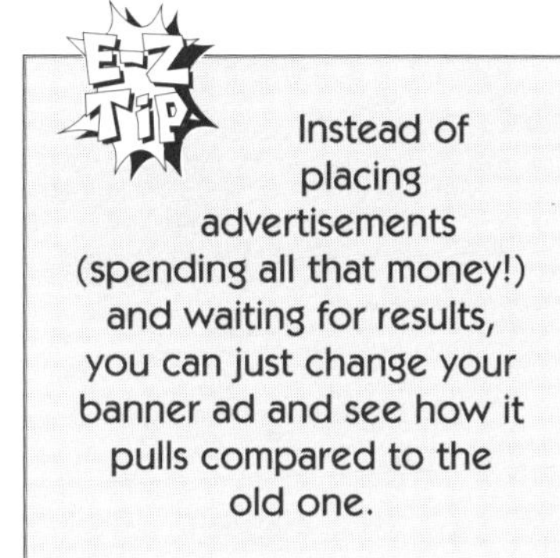

So, I changed the ad slightly to say "money making and money saving reports" instead of "business and consumer reports":

FREE!!	Click Here for HUNDREDS of Money-Making and Money-Saving Reports —Read them online. Free!

I anxiously waited until enough people viewed the new banner to make a fair comparison, then I checked my stats again. Of the 2,321 people that saw new banner, 24 of them clicked on it to visit my site. That meant with the new banner, it only took 96 people seeing the ad to get one to visit. That's better than a 2:1 improvement over the first one!

Woohoo! That little change DOUBLED the effectiveness of the ad. And guess what it cost me to test this out? Try $0.00! If you have a site with a good amount of traffic, you could conceivably test several different ads in a single day.

Now, I bet you're wondering about that "sneaky way" of getting click-thru ratios of 10:1 (or better), aren't you? Take a look at this banner:

See how sneaky it is? If you are familiar with web pages, you recognize that this picture looks like a Windows list box. I am certain that many people click on that little arrow fully expecting to get a list box, and instead they are transported to another web site. I know that has happened to me a few times before I caught on. Sneaky! I personally don't want to trick people into coming to my site, but it's up to you. No doubt you *will* get more people to visit your site that way.

Search engines and directories

DEFINITION

How do people find what they want to on the Internet? Through the use of a search engine of course. A *search engine* is a web site dedicated to helping people find what they are looking for on the Internet. Think of them as "phone books and indices" for the Internet.

There are several search engines, and they all do things a little bit differently. For instance, Yahoo! puts all known web sites into a hierarchical organization. If you wanted to search for sites related to "pottery," you could enter the keyword "pottery" and click on the "SEARCH" button. Yahoo! would list several categories:

1) Business and Economy: Companies: Arts and Crafts: Visual Arts: Ceramics

2) Society and Culture: Cultures and Groups: Cultures: Native American: Art

3) Business and Economy: Companies: Entertainment: Video: Tape Sales: Titles (this category had a site offering a video of 18th century pottery techniques—how fascinating)

4) Business and Economy: Companies: Arts and Crafts: Supplies and Equipment: Ceramic

5) and several others

What if you want to look up art sites, but weren't sure what particular kind of art you were looking for? You could just start browsing the site, by clicking on "art." On the resulting page, you could click on the category "Visual Art," then "Ceramics," and finally "Index—Potter's Page, The." You see, with Yahoo you don't have to know exactly what you're looking for; just browse until something of interest catches your eye.

> **note** All the search engines allow you to do a search on keywords; some also have indices by subject category.

Enter the words describing your interest, and hit the "go search" button. In seconds you are given a page full of (hopefully) relevant links. Click on a link and you're immediately whisked to some far corner of the internet universe. The sheer volume of information at your fingertips is astounding.

Other sites work differently—Alta Vista is known for its huge number of indexed words/pages. Other pages allow you to do multiple searches in many different search engines at the same time. Some even filter out duplicate pages, or sift through search results to filter out some of the chaff.

Your best use of search engines is for research. This is especially useful if you are creating an "information product." I mentioned information products in earlier, and if that's not what you're into, that's okay, but you may want to create some of your own short and simple information products to use as customer incentives, giveaways, etc. I'm just talking about simple 3 to 10 page reports, like something you did in school. I digress. More on this subject later.

As I said, search engines are MADE for research, but you should also do everything you can to get your web page into the search engines. It doesn't cost anything, and remember, this is the first place people go when they look for something on the Internet. More about the "how to" of this in the Internet Marketing section.

1-900 order placement

This is just one more option you can give your customers for placing an order for your software product. Originally, this service was designed with the following process in mind:

1) Your prospect downloads (or receives from a friend) a *shareware* version of your software. The software would be created in such a way that additional features are made available entering a registration code.

2) After deciding to register (purchase) the software (and thus obtain the additional features), the customer calls a 1-900 number which charges a specified price to their phone bill. They are given a PIN number by way of a recording at this number.

3) The customer enters the PIN number in a web page (form).

4) The service checks the PIN number against their list of valid numbers, and if it is valid, they forward the customer information to you.

5) You send the customer the special registration code via e-mail.

Though originally intended for registration of shareware computer software, this service can also be used for outright purchases. Instead of supplying the customer with a registration code, you send the actual program via e-mail, or tell them how to get into a password protected area of your site to download the software.

This company charges a commission of 20% + $1.00. They only allow 10 different price points. They have a different 1-900 number for each price.

Here are the prices and how much you would keep for each sale:

Your Price	You Keep (after commission)
$4.95	$2.96
$5.95	$3.76
$7.95	$5.36
$10.00	$7.00
$12.00	$8.60
$15.00	$11.00
$19.95	$14.96
$25.00	$19.00
$30.00	$23.00
$35.00	$27.00

As always, check the Resource Chapter for contact information.

3

More powerful tools to boost your profits

Chapter 3

More powerful tools to boost your profits

What you'll find in this chapter:

- Testing your advertising
- Classified ads and e-zines
- Pointers for good ad writing
- Direct mail opportunities
- The Internet retail store

Okay, now that you have all these tools available to you, what do you do with them? How can you use them to secure more leads and orders?

Even though the tools in Chapter Two are new, your goals are the same—to communicate with your prospects and customers in order to get more sales. These tools are just new ways of achieving that goal. As such, some of the "conventional" methods are more suited to using these new tools than others.

The methods I am talking about are classified ads, display advertising, and direct mail. Though an exhaustive treatment of each of these methods is beyond the scope of this guide (several books are written about each of these topics), I will show you the fundamentals. I also provide references to other books about the methods you are most interested in pursuing.

If you study these fundamentals, apply them, and test your advertisements like you should, you'll be successful. The effort you exert in studying and applying additional material about these methods determines the *extent* of your success.

While some of the tools discussed in Chapter Two are only available through use of the Internet, they can be used in all aspects of your marketing, not just Internet marketing. Likewise, many of the methods used in conventional advertising mediums work equally well in the Internet channels.

For these reasons, my discussion of the various methods does not differentiate between Internet and conventional marketing. Direct marketing is salesmanship, no matter whether your message is seen on a computer monitor, in a glossy magazine, or on standard 20-pound bond paper. A classified ad is a classified ad whether run in a paper magazine or an e-zine. The principles are the same.

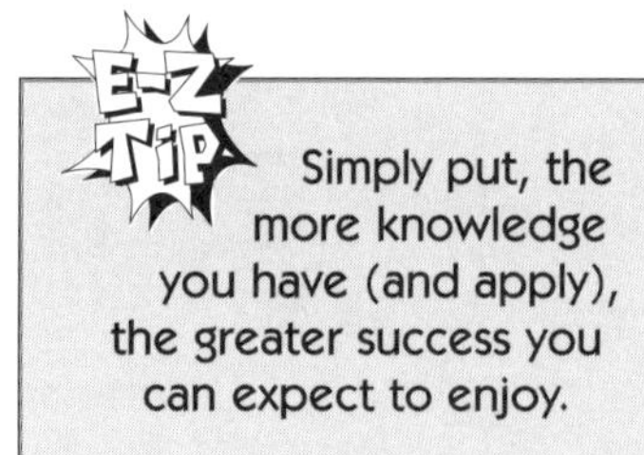

Even in light of the above statement, there are some unique promotional requirements for marketing on the Internet, which is why I also devoted a chapter to the discussion of Internet marketing.

> CAUTION
> Keep in mind that what worked well with one offer a year ago may not work so well with a different offer (or even the same offer!) now.

A word of caution: The methods and techniques discussed here are based on the results obtained by several successful marketers. But, you still need to do your own testing! Just because someone is an expert, doesn't mean you shouldn't put their advice to the test! Don't jump in headfirst just on the word of some guru. Test the water a little before you dive. If you don't, believe me, there will come a day when you'll regret it.

Notes about testing

Before we get into the different advertising methods, let's briefly discuss testing that is required for all of them.

Keying ads

In order to determine where your orders are coming from (so you can see what works and what doesn't), you need to *key* your ad. This means doing something slightly different in the response mechanism.

If your customer orders by phone, use a different extension or item number in each ad. Or, if they order by fax or mail, place a different item number on the ordering coupon. Keying your ads is critical!

You don't want to continue spending money on ads that aren't generating orders. You want to discontinue those ads and roll more advertising dollars into the ads that *are* making money. This is true for using different ads in the same medium as well as for using the same ad in different mediums—key everything.

Analyzing results

All that really matters is the bottom line—profit! Some outdated thinking is that you need at least a 2% response rate to your direct mail piece to be profitable. But, what if you are selling a $200 item that costs you $6.00 including fulfillment? (By the way, such products DO exist—usually they are information products or software.) Unless you have extremely high mailings costs, you make a nice profit at less than 1% response.

The same goes for classified and display advertisements. Some marketing books maintain that the important performance measurement is the *cost per lead (CPL).* They further state that you should shoot for a CPL of $1.00 or less. Let's say you got a CPL of $3.33 each—on a $100 ad cost, that would mean you got 30 requests for more information. If you could convert 10 of those requests into $2,5.00 orders, at a product and fulfillment cost of $4.00 each, would that be a profitable ad? Let's see:

Costs:	
Advertisement	**$100.00**
Mail sales letter (report) to 30 inquiries	**$ 15.00**
Product and fulfillment costs of 10 orders	**$ 40.00**
Total	**$155.00**
Revenue:	
10 orders @ $25/order	**$250.00**
Profit:	**$ 95.00**

Yes, that's profitable all right!

Always look at the bottom line when evaluating the success of your marketing efforts. The other numbers can be useful. If you find a way to lower your CPL, great, so much the better. But, the goal of your ad isn't to get a CPL of $1.00, the GOAL is to make a profit. You could offer a free book that costs you $2.00 to everyone that called your 1-800 number, and you'd probably get a boatload of inquiries, but at what cost? Your CPL would be low, but your costs would be high, and you could lose your shirt. Don't lose sight of the big picture.

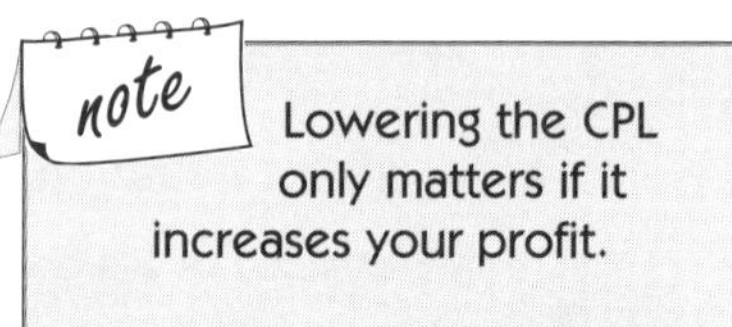

Closely related to this is the issue of *correct* analysis. If I ran an advertisement in a popular, large circulation magazine, got one order, and lost $1,421 on the whole campaign, what would that say about my ad? Wouldn't you think the ad was a dismal failure? Perhaps. But, what if you learned that I would run the ad in *Men's Health* magazine, and it was an ad for "How to keep your legs perfectly hair-free and smooth 100% of the time—in just 30 seconds each day." Wouldn't you then think the problem was with my selection of the ad medium—NOT with the ad itself? Of course.

Granted, that was an obvious example, but I think it illustrates the point. Here's another (less obvious) example. Say you had used a particular sales letter with great success on a test batch of 5,000 names from a mailing list. You then mailed to an additional 15,000 names from the same list, but with much lower response!

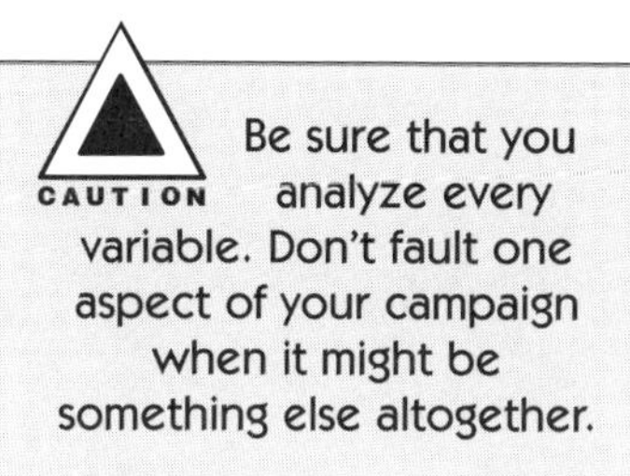

Naturally, your first inclination is to blame the list. "That rotten list dealer gave me good names for my test and then gave me junk names for my main rollout." (By the way, this scenario DOES happen in real life.)

However, upon further examination, you might find that you forgot to change the offer expiration date in your sales letter, or on the ordering coupon. Or, perhaps the company you use for mailing services inadvertently used BULK RATE instead of the first class postage that you specified.

There are so many variables in every marketing campaign. Be sure you have all the facts before you draw any conclusions. The wrong conclusions will run in circles at best, and could ultimately lead your business to failure.

A note for storefront retail business owners

If you're operating a storefront or office based business, where you must meet with customers/clients face to face, you may think that this kind of advertising (classifieds, display ads, direct mail) doesn't apply to you. Don't close your mind to it. Many traditional consumer oriented businesses (carpet cleaning, financial planning, insurance, etc.) produced extraordinary results by using non-traditional direct marketing techniques.

If you are only using yellow-page ads and cooperative mailings, you severely limit yourself! Even if you use radio and TV, you can still benefit from these methods. Some of these methods can be successfully applied to your current advertising as well. What is a yellow-page ad anyway? A display ad, of course.

If you are one of these people, you should create your own report, kit, cassette, video, or some other information product that you can offer to respondents of your classified and display advertisements. Don't panic, it doesn't have to be a 100 page book, it can be as small as a 3 to 4 page report, but it must contain useful information.

For instance, consider a company that wants to sell a bi-weekly mortgage plan to new homeowners. Their report outline might be something like this:

1) Congratulations on your new home (introduction)
2) With your 30 year mortgage, you pay $18,6432.16 in interest (make them feel the pain!)
3) If you decide to move in 5 years, you only have $4,215 in equity—less than what it costs to sell your house (more pain!)
4) Biweekly payments will:
    - cut interest by $58,079.00
    - allow you to payoff loan 7 years earlier
    - increase equity after 5 years by $5,000.00
5) We can help you with your biweekly program
    - no appraisal needed
    - no credit check required
    - no refinancing mess
6) Free mortgage auditing for our biweekly clients
7) Start accelerating your equity now

All this could be done quite professionally with equity versus time graphs, amortization tables, etc. Chances are that the company has all this information already. They just need to put it in a free report or a mortgage reduction kit, or something similar.

If you are a car mechanic, create a report about the common ways dishonest mechanics rip-off their customers and what people can to do make sure they aren't a victim of these unscrupulous characters.

If you own a video store . . . hmm, that's a bit different . . . how about this: Offer parents a report of the newest family-oriented videos. This report changes as you receive different videos, and includes reviews/recommendations, some trivia about the actors, etc. That involves a little more effort than some of the previous examples, but I bet you would be the only one offering such a service.

If you just can't stand the thought of creating a short information product for lead-generation, consider having a college student do it. It is easier than most English projects they were assigned in the past! Get that report made somehow; you must have something you can offer the readers of your advertisements.

If you are advertising to a local market, you may just offer this information product (and perhaps a discount?) to people who come in and visit you. It doesn't have to be sent through the mail.

As you read the following pages, keep an open mind and look for ways that to apply these methods to your own situation. You will be pleasantly surprised at the number of profit-building ideas you dream up!

Classified ads

Ah, the lowly classified ad. The stuff legends are made of. If you've been on an opportunity seekers mailing list for any length of time, I have no doubt you've seen a number of sales letters for books or reports that showed you "How to get rich with classified ads," or something similar. Am I right?

Well, the truth is classifieds do work, if you know how to use them. On a dollar for dollar basis, they can't be beat as an advertising medium. The disadvantage, is they can't be used for "One-Step" advertising. You won't make any money if you ask for the order from a classified ad—it takes a lot more information than that to overcome people's skepticism and convince them to part with their hard earned dollars.

Your goal should be to get the *qualified* reader to ask for more information. By this I mean you don't want to spend your time and money sending free information to every tire kicker, every collector of free information, but to spend them on true potential customers. Some people send for every free thing they can get, just to get stuff in the mail. Don't laugh, it's true. More on this in a bit.

When using classifieds, the conventional approach has been the following:

- *You place a classified advertisement,* and the reader responds with a request for more information—usually a free report, free kit, etc., either by mail or by leaving their name/address on a voice mail system.

- *You send the report* (which includes your offer) to everyone that requests the information. If they like what they read—if your information is good—and they want to take advantage of your offer, they place an order.

If you're a retail establishment advertising to the local market, you might opt to use the voice mail recording to invite people to come in for their free report, or for a free video, or whatever you're offering. You need to run your own tests to see which method is best—sending them something in the mail or just having them come in to get it.

If you use print advertising, I highly recommend using voice mail as your response vehicle. People don't want to go through the trouble and extra time associated with responding by mail—and it always pays to make things easy for your prospects! In fact, the majority of advertisers now list a phone number instead of an address, since prospects take the path of least resistance in almost every case.

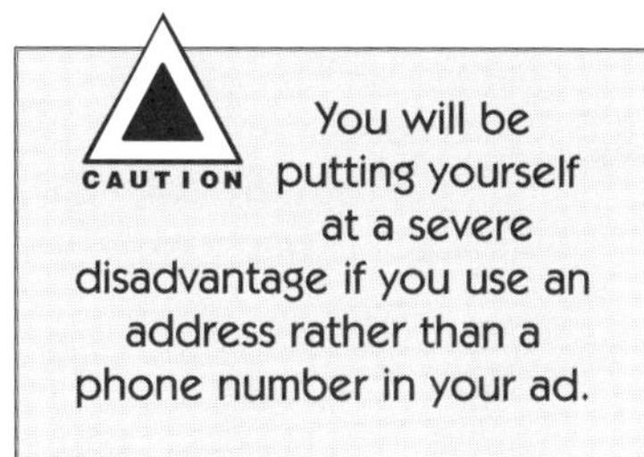

If you are advertising in an Internet publication (newsletter, e-zine, etc.) you have several additional options. You could have the person reply to your e-mail, or you have them reply to your autoresponder which would be a totally automatic solution. You could also direct them to a page on your web site designed to get their e-mail and/or regular mail address. Or, have them send an e-mail to your list-server "subscribe" e-mail address.

Some very successful Internet marketers swear by "taking the prospect away from the Internet"—make the prospect pick up the phone and call a number. This forces the prospect to see your offer as part of the real world rather than the virtual world of the Internet. It is also advantageous to get a real *paper* sales letter (report) in their hands, and this lends credibility to your company. Anyone can produce a web page and publish their e-mail address. Never has it been so easy to be here today, gone tomorrow than with the Internet!

Place your ads in publications having several ads similar to your own. Now, that may sound strange to some people—why not place the ad somewhere with no competing ads? The reason is because if a publication doesn't have similar ads to yours, it is usually because people tried running that kind of ad, and it was a flop. If you see several ads similar to yours—running week after week, month after month—then you know that kind of ad is successful in that publication.

As you can tell from the previous paragraph, you need to do some research when determining where to run your ad. Go to your nearest library and look at the back issues for the publication of interest. If the e-zine has a web site, their archives will be there. If you cannot find back issues or archives of the publication you are evaluating for your own ads, you just need to collect a few issues of your own. This requires patience on your part, but don't skip this critical step.

Once you have the back issues and/or archives of the publications of interest, look at their classified ad section. Have ads similar to yours been running in that publication for several months? The best indicator is if a particular ad is repeated every issue for several weeks or months—that means the advertiser is making money! If he's making money with his ad in that publication, you'll make money too—if you have a good ad (which we talk about later), sales letter, or product.

Remember when I was talking about modeling other successful operations? When you find these ads that are run continuously, you really

SHOULD answer them and study the sales letter, or product of that company. If you do this, and if you do what they do conceptually (I'm not talking about copying their sales material), then you should be successful too.

If you are going to advertise in print media, test your ad first in your local "penny saver" or neighborhood papers, as long as they have ads similar to the one you want to run. Advertisements get more attention in a neighborhood paper than they do in the daily papers.

Remember when I said you want qualified readers to ask for more information? This means you don't want all the tire kickers to answer your ad, but you do want the people most likely to buy your product to ask more about it. So how can your ad act as a filter? There are a couple of ways.

First, do not, I repeat, DO NOT use a toll-free number!

"What, doesn't that violate the rule of making things easy on your customer?! Won't they be more likely to call if it doesn't cost them anything?"

Yes to both questions, BUT in this case, that's okay. If someone is really interested in what you offer, they'll make the toll call. If they're not interested enough to pay the few cents for the call, you don't want to waste your time and money. You greatly reduce your risk this way too—1-800 per-minute charges can eat you alive.

If you have the financial wherewithal for it, go ahead and run a test. Run one ad with a 1-800 number and another ad without. Then, see how the profit picture looks for both ads. At least when you start out, stick with the "qualify the responses" toll call method.

The second way to qualify people is to use a specific ad rather than a generic one. Compare these two ads:

> Make money from home! $300 for 4 hours work! Call 555-555-5555 (recording) for free report!
>
> You can make $300 in 4 hours trading currency with your home computer! Call 555-555-5555 (recording) for free report!

Notice how the second ad tells the reader more specific information. Will your product be of any use to anyone who doesn't have a computer at home? Nope! So, you don't want a bunch of people without computers asking for more information, do you? Will this ad appeal to anyone who is looking specifically for an opportunity in a service business? Again, no.

This ad will only be answered by people interested in making money by trading currency on the foreign exchange market, with their home computer. Those are the people you want to send information to, not all the tire kicking something-for-nothing opportunity seekers.

> note
>
> While you may get fewer responses to a very specific ad, the responses will be of much higher quality.

An exception to this rule is when you use an Internet classified ad coupled with an autoresponder as your response mechanism. In this case, it doesn't matter WHO or HOW MANY people respond to your ad, the cost is the same. That's the beauty of Internet advertising—it's quick and so very inexpensive. If you are advertising on the Internet, and using an autoresponder to send more information to your respondents, there is no financial risk with using a nonspecific ad.

On the other hand, if you reply to the respondents by conventional mail (taking the prospect away from the Internet, remember?), you still want to use a specific advertisement and deal only with qualified leads.

If you were observant, you noticed that in all my example classified advertisements, I place "(recording)" after the phone number. This is because people are more likely to call if they know they won't be dealing with a high-pressure sales person. A recording is not a threat, and you have many more responses by letting the readers know that is what they get when they call. You may have also noticed that I always offer a free report. This sounds much more valuable than free details, wouldn't you agree?

Now, how do you WRITE a good classified ad? Believe it or not, whole books are written on the subject, but here's enough for you to get started.

First of all, the length of your classified ad is somewhat dependent on the publication you advertising in. Most publications require you to pay for a minimum number of words. If you use fewer than that many words, you still pay the minimum. If you use more, you pay an additional charge for every word over the minimum number.

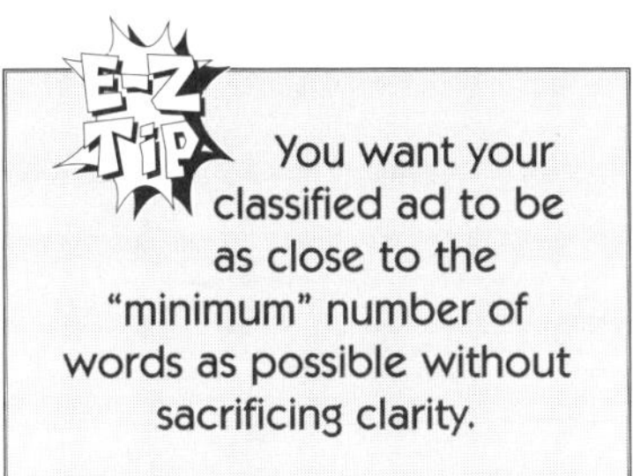

If you recall from our discussion of headlines, a headline should stand on its own—in other words, a headline should be able to make it as a classified ad. So, when creating your classified ad, that's where you should start—create a headline for your product/service sales message.

If you have your sales letter prepared, and if you did what I told you to do when creating your headline, then you should have several headlines that you can use as classified advertisements—just tack on " . . . call 555-555-5555 (recording) for free report!" or something similar. Use the most powerful headline that comes closest to the minimum number of words. If you only have short headlines, and you have several words to spare, you want to use two of your headlines or more (some modification might be required to maintain a good flow).

When we talked about headlines, you didn't know that you were writing classified ads, did you?

This is also a perfect place to use your swipe file. As you collect long-running classified ads, you are able to analyze these ads and see what key words keep popping up. Don't EVER copy someone else's ad word for word. But, you MUST model your ads after other successful ads by using the same key words. No one has a monopoly on the words *Free* or *You* (both very powerful), or any other words. Create your ad from a combination of the power words you see in other ads. I listed some of these power words in the Reference Chapter, they may prove helpful as well.

You want your classified ad to be as benefit-laden as possible. Some classifieds are so short that all you have room for is the headline; others are much longer. Some Internet classified ad minimums are 100 words. Regardless the length, you need to get every facet of the AIDA formula in your ad.

This may seem like an oversimplified explanation of how to write a classified ad, but there really isn't much to it, especially if you do what you should—study the successful ads of others and model yours after theirs. One direct marketing expert stated that a 12 year old could write a classified, and he's right. The secret behind that truth is the methodical study of other successful advertisements.

note

If you list every benefit (not feature) of your product/service, you should have plenty of material to pull from when creating your ad.

Timing your ad

One thing I haven't talked about is *when* to place your classified advertisements. Some say that the summer months are dreadful for direct response marketing. Others claim great success during these months. Some have bad experiences when advertising in December, but for others it is their best month. Sorry, my friend, there is no easy answer on this one, there are too many variables. You need to conduct your own tests!

If your product or service is something you can offer in weekly newspapers and/or shopper publications on a national or statewide scale, (after you did some thorough TESTING), there are some organizations that make your life much easier. Rather than going through the time and expense of contacting every publication in your state (or the country) individually, you can use the services of these organizations. You can place ONE order, and have your ad in anywhere from 40 to over 4,000 papers—at a much reduced cost when compared to doing it all yourself, one paper at a time.

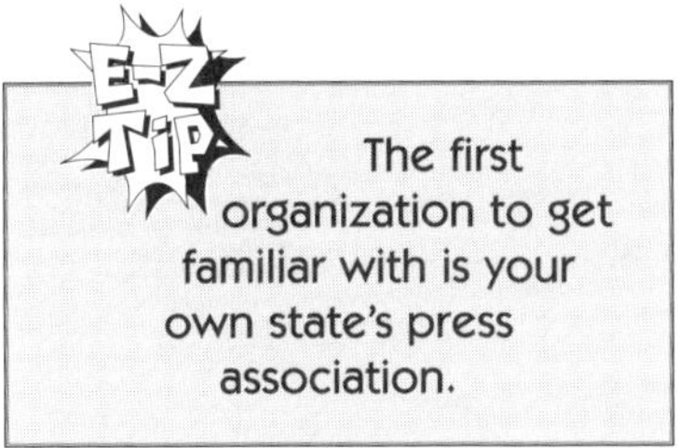

Press associations were created for the express purpose of helping people and businesses place ads in papers throughout the state. They represent anywhere from 23 up to 300 newspapers (dailies and weeklies). To place an ad in all the papers they represent, you only need to send the ad with payment to the press association. The rates are lower than if you place the ad with each paper individually. For instance, to place your 25 word ad in over 300 Texas newspapers, (265 weeklies) it costs you just $300.00—that's about 4 cents per word, per paper. Remember, most of these papers are small town weekly or neighborhood papers, which are much better for most ads in the first place.

Don't get so excited about this that you fail to properly test your ad in the local weeklies before rolling out. You must be sure you have a winner ad that appeals to the readers of this type of paper before risking your hard earned dollars on a statewide campaign.

Once you have an ad that proves successful in a statewide campaign, you can branch out into other states. It isn't necessary to contact each state press association individually. Your state's association can process your order for the papers in other states as well because they all have an agreement with each other that allows for this convenience.

Contact information for the state press associations is in the resource material. There are three companies with similar and complementary services listed there too. Check them out!

Display ads

I'm going to be straight up honest with you—I don't use display advertising much, and that being the case, I don't consider myself an authority on it. What I can do is pass along some commonly accepted knowledge about display advertising and suggest how some of the new tools discussed in Chapter Two can be used with display advertising. If you are interested in direct marketing, there are some fine books listed in the Reference Chapter that teach you all you need to know.

As far as message lengths go, the display advertisement falls solidly between classified ads and sales letters. There is enough room in a full page display advertisement (a GOOD advertisement) to profitably sell items costing less than $30. Items below $20 fare even better. Less expensive items can be sold directly from smaller ads. However, profitable one-step display advertising is getting harder all the time because the advertising costs are just too darn high!

For this reason, many marketers don't really expect to profit from the "front-end" orders, but they make up for it in subsequent orders. Or, they don't even try to sell anything with the initial display advertisement, they just use a two step approach like we discussed with classifieds. In fact, with display ads smaller than one-half to full-page size, this is generally the only way to do things.

Typical "dial-up" Internet accounts don't yet have the speed that makes display advertising very practical. There are banner ads, sure, but they are more like glorified classifieds than display ads, so I wouldn't recommend posting a large display ad in any Internet forums—it just wouldn't get much readership.

With a display advertisement, you have room to include testimonials. In fact, a strong testimonial could be a great headline. You also have room to list several different options for people that want more information. Joe Schroeder's MLM ads are grcat examples of this. In his ad he usually has one or two "tele-seminar" phone numbers, fax-on-demand number, voice mail number, and perhaps even a 1-800 number you can call to hear a short motivational message. I also saw display ads that list fax-on-demand, e-mail, voice-mail, web site, and auto-responder information.

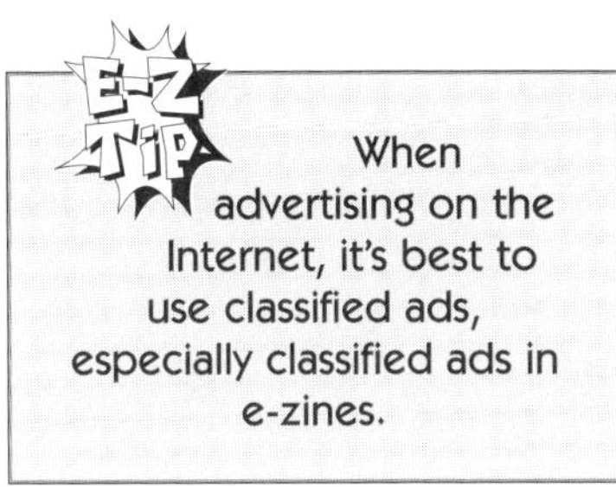

One clever trick I saw was an ad that listed several fax document codes along with a fax-on-demand number. Of course, they instructed people to leave a voice mail message if they wanted the free information, but didn't have a fax machine.

The best advertisement you'll ever have in a magazine or newspaper is not really an advertisement at all. That's right! A favorable review of your product done by someone working at the paper brings in more orders and/or leads than any paid advertisement (see the section on free publicity). The more you can make your advertisement look like an objective third-party review or editorial, the better. Try to use the same font and format used in the news copy of the publication you advertise in, and make the headline "newsy"—something that COULD be a news story headline. This kind of ad is commonly referred to as an *advertorial.* One of the best examples of this is the half-page ad for golf balls with this headline:

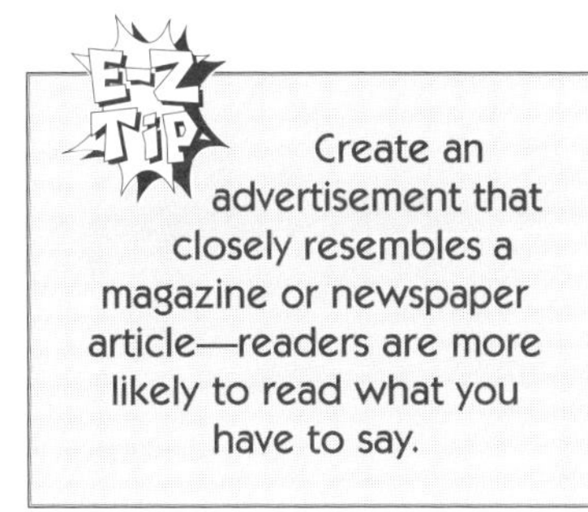

"Golf Pros Banned From Using New 'Hot' Ball; Flies Too Far"

Except for the obligatory "Advertisement" heading placed there by the magazine, this advertisement looks and reads like a news story. I've seen it in many magazines and in many books about how to write ads.

While trying to determine what I would write about the "how-to" of display advertising, I discovered most of the good stuff was already in the first chapter of this guide, under "copywriting." So first, I direct you to read that section again. Re-acquaint yourself with the basics like motivation, AIDA, and emotion versus logic. Then come back here.

Back already? Now here are a few pointers specifically for display advertising:

- **Pictures:** Contrary to what we naturally expect, pictures do not always improve the performance of a display advertisement. Unless the picture is demonstrating the benefits that come with the use of the product (like a closet organizer, for instance), it can actually HURT your ad response. Rather than play hit and miss with a picture, spend some extra time coming up with a super headline. After your advertisement proves successful, you may want to do some testing with a picture added. If you DO use a picture, be sure to include a caption beneath it. The caption should hit on a major benefit which is clearly demonstrated in the picture. Captions have a very high readership.

- **Stress benefits, not features:** I know I covered that before, but I want to give it some added emphasis. *Benefits, benefits, benefits!* Remember, start your benefit list with "You will . . ." or "You get . . ." (not necessarily printed out, but in your head start them this way). That forces you to write "you" advertising rather than "me" advertising.

- **Use Dropped Capitals:** According to Ted Nicholas, your advertisement gets a better response if you start the first paragraph of your ad body with a dropped capital letter. I've never done the test of using this versus not using it, but if Ted Nicholas says it helps, it's a good place to start. As always, do your own testing.

- **Strong Guarantee Required:** If you are placing a "one-step" ad, a strong guarantee is especially important. The longer the guarantee, the more credibility you give yourself and the fewer returns you get. Why is this? Well, think about it. If you only have 7 days to look something over and return it, that's going to be your top priority, right? Plus, you are so worried about missing the return deadline, that your evaluation of the product may be rushed. In fact, if you're too pressed for time, you may return it without even checking it out. Giving a long guarantee allows your prospect/customer to relax.

- **Impulse vs. Analysis:** What was written in the copywriting section about having a sales message that appealed to impulsive as well as to analytical readers applies doubly to your display advertisements.

> **E-Z TIP** Break up your copy with sub-headlines, bulleted lists, one sentence paragraphs, one word sentences . . . so a "scanner" can get the gist of what you're offering, but also include details for people who want them.

You should definitely study your swipe file advertisements long and hard when you create your own display ads. Follow the lead of those who were there already, made (and paid for) mistakes, learned from them, and ultimately were successful. More than anything else, studying the successful ads of other marketers helps you to create your own profitable ads.

If this chapter is the only thing you ever read about display advertising, and if you want to USE display advertising for your own business, do yourself a favor. Go to the library and check out some of the books on copywriting recommended in the References/Resources Chapter. This little bit you read here isn't enough.

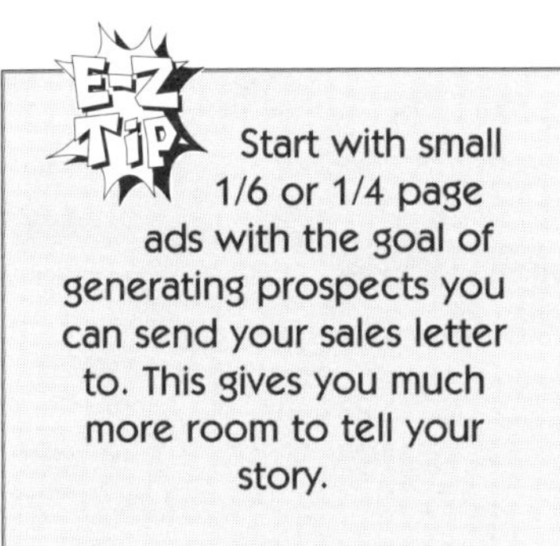

As an aside, no matter how much you read, you learn the most when you finally place your own advertisement, analyze the results, make changes, and try again. The hardest thing is to take that first step, stick your neck (wallet!) out and see what happens. There comes a time when you need to write your first classified and/or display advertisement and/or sales letter—doing the best you know how, and using the knowledge you have. Then run a small test, see what happens, make appropriate adjustments, and do it again!

The beauty of this business is that you don't have to risk thousands of dollars running your tests. You can run a classified ad for a few dollars, place a small display ad for $250, or mail a letter to 1,000 people for $500. Don't analyze and study everything to death, just get out and DO IT!

CAUTION Some people spend thousands of dollars buying books and tapes, going to seminars, watching information videos . . . but they never DO anything. Don't get caught in that trap!

Direct mail

When you place a classified or display advertisement, you have a limited amount of space to use in convincing the reader to take action. When using direct mail, you aren't hindered in this manner—you can say as much as you need to, and you can use written words, pictures, even audio or video if you want. So, why not use direct mail exclusively? Cost. Mailing a bad offer or mailing a good offer to a bad list (very easily done!) can put you out of business almost before you get started. Of course, direct *e-mail* is an exception to this, isn't it? Good thing, too.

The best lists to mail to are:

- current customers
- inactive customers
- prospects who have recently requested information (usually in response to your display or classified advertisement)
- buyers of products/services similar to your own

If you're just starting out, you'll spend all your time obtaining new customers. However, as you establish a customer base you should shift more and more of your efforts towards developing your relationship with them. The most expensive sale is to the new customer. Once someone buys from you and is DELIGHTED with your customer service and product, they trust you and will buy from you again, and again, and again. As long as you keep delivering on the promised benefits, they'll keep buying!

This implies, of course, that you have additional products and/or services to offer someone once they become your customer—and I hope you do. Remember, the back end is where you make all your profit. This is where your return on investment can be 5, 8, 20, even 100 times what you invest! Imagine spending $250 on a test mailing to your current customers and receiving $5,000 in return—this isn't extraordinary by any means. For some marketers it's almost commonplace.

> **note** The majority (at least 70%) of your marketing efforts should be concentrated on your existing customers.

Business owners are sometimes too timid—they are afraid that if they mail offers to their customer base too often, their customers will get annoyed and stop buying. Don't fall into this trap of lost sales. Mail to your customers frequently—a minimum of once per month. Now, don't mail to them just for the sake of mailing—make them genuine, high value, high benefit offers with each mailing. One time it may be a 20% discount offer, the next time it may be a free bonus offer, or a free 2 day/3 night travel certificate. If you have a retail store, invite them to an "after hours, current customer only" sale. Use every excuse (new-product announcements, anniversaries, holidays, spring, summer, back-to-school, etc.) to give them a special offer.

> **note**
> Some people you mail to may be annoyed and will ask you to quit pestering them. The great majority will appreciate your frequent offers.

Much of what you do for current customers can also be used with inactive customers—customers that haven't ordered for 90 days or whatever time frame you specify. It varies depending on your business.

When a prospect requests more information, don't waste any time getting it to them. When they request it is when they are the most likely to BUY. Send it within 24 hours of receiving their request. Depending on the cost/profit picture of your product/service, try following up with additional letters and/or phone calls. Some businesses use *series letters*—a series of three to seven (or more) letters they send at regular intervals after an inquiry is received. The higher priced your offer, the more likely it is that you'll profit from this kind of strategy.

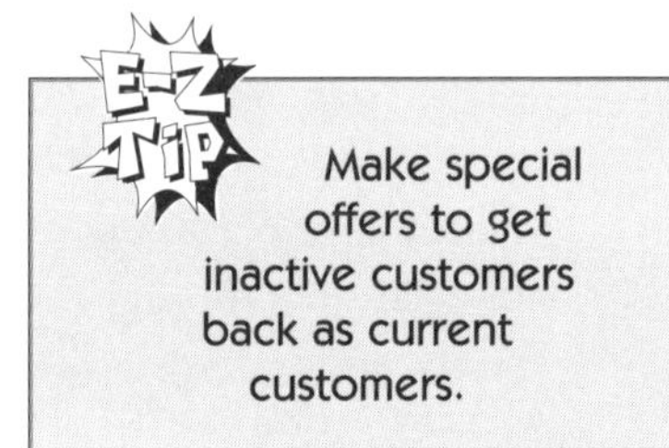

So far we talked about mailing lists that you generated from your own efforts. There are also lists you can mail to that were generated by the efforts of others. Depending on the source, these can be very profitable lists, or they can be a big waste of money. That's why you TEST them before blowing your whole marketing budget!

If you have a product that complements someone else's, you may be able to arrange a joint venture mailing with them. As an example, say you offered a biweekly payment service for mortgage holders. You convince a mortgage or real-estate company to enter into a venture where they mail your offer to their customer list with a cover letter from them extolling the virtues of your service. This accomplishes two things:

1) More customers OPEN the envelope because they recognize the name—it's their mortgage company, so who would throw that away without looking at it? (Okay, I know we would all like to pretend we didn't have a mortgage, but we know better than to try.)

2) Once they open it, they get a glowing recommendation from someone they trust and did business with before—a recommendation for YOUR service!

After all costs of mailing are paid, you split the remaining profit with your partner. Sure, your profits per sale aren't as high, but you get a lot more sales than if you sent your offer without that trust-building cover letter.

It works the other way too. If someone else has a product that complements YOURS, why not enter a joint venture with them? They take all the risk associated with the mailing, you have nothing to lose. Make sure they have a quality product and excellent customer service, since you don't want another company's shortcomings to reflect badly on you.

Now, if you absolutely must, you can mail to *cold* lists. These are "buyers lists" that you rent from a list broker. If you were selling a CD Cleaner Kit for instance, you might be interested in purchasing a list of buyers of CDs from the *Columbia CD Club*. Or, if you're selling a video course on how to fly-fish, you might want to rent the names of subscribers to *Field and Stream* magazine.

The better you can match the previously purchased product to your own, the better the list will work for you. If you have a $75 item, you will probably have better results with a list of people that bought a $100 item in the past than with a list of people that bought a $19 item.

If you're going to rent a list, you need to become intimately familiar with the Standard Rate and Data Service (SRDS) publication *Direct Marketing List Source.*. This resource has thousands of listings in over 200 categories. These categories are listed in the Reference/Resource Chapter, just looking at them may give you some great ideas for your own marketing!

The SRDS publications are expensive—hundreds of dollars for a yearly subscription—but they are also available at libraries. You may also be able to talk an acquaintance at an advertising agency to give you an old copy when the new one arrives. However you do it, you need to become familiar with this resource and the mailing lists in it.

Tom Mudry's first book *Direct Mail & Direct Response Advertising Techniques the "EXPERTS" Don't Want you to Know About!* discusses the proper use of the direct marketing list source in great detail. If you're going to use direct mail to these kinds of lists, I highly recommend you get a copy. It's listed in the Reference/Resource Chapter (you knew I was going to say that, didn't you?)

There are some nasty tricks some unethical list brokers play on the unwary, so watch out! When you test a list, you should ask your broker for every "nth name". Say that a mailing list contained 50000 names, but you only wanted to do a test of 2000 names. 50,000 ÷ 2000 = 25, so you'd ask your broker to give you every 25th name—that way you have a good sampling of the whole list. By the way, you may have a difficult time finding a list owner/broker willing to rent fewer than 5,000 names at once—rent the 5,000 names (you ask for a 10th name selection in the above example) but only mail to 1,000 or 2,000 of them for your first test.

One of the most common schemes is to give you "cream of the crop" names for your test mailing , rather than every 25th name as you requested. Then your test results are fantastic, and they offer you a "special deal" on the rest of the names. When you roll out to the remaining names, your response isn't even half as good as in your test, and you lose your shirt.

Another ruse some brokers play is to give you names that aren't as recent as advertised, or they tell you that the people on the list made purchases of $25 to $50 each, when in reality they only spent $5-$15 in past purchases. Always test as you go, don't get impatient and mail to the whole list.

One other low-cost, low-risk possibility is to have your sales material included in a "package stuffer" program. If you had a fitness-related product or service, your sales material might be well received if it was placed in the shipping box for someone who ordered one of those exercise machines from the television commercials. Costs for this type of distribution is around $40 per thousand inserts—dirt cheap compared to sending a mailing! Several of these programs are listed in the direct marketing list source. Go to your library and examine this great resource. Make sure you have a couple of hours to spend, because there is a lot there.

> **E-Z TIP** Once you mailed your test names, don't mail to all the remaining names at once; mail to a portion of the names and see how your response is. If it's good, then mail to a few thousand more. Keep up this "mail and evaluate" routine until the list has been used.

Though I discussed copywriting fundamentals in Chapter One, here are a few more tips related to the sales letter itself:

- **The first thing your customer should see:** The HEADLINE. Don't bore the customer with your corporate letterhead and logo—that's not "you" advertising. The first thing the customer should see is a headline that emphasizes a major benefit for them. There are always exceptions to this rule, as with all others. If you are a professional organization mailing to other professionals (doctor to doctor, lawyer to lawyer, etcetera), your letterhead may cause more people to read the rest of the letter. As always, TEST.

- **Always use a P.S. in your sales letters:** After the headline, the P.S. of your sales letter is read more than anything else. ALWAYS have a P.S., and make sure that it emphasizes a strong benefit. You may also want a "call to action" here, or a "reason to act now."

- **End pages with a broken sentence:** When you get to the end of a page in your sales letter, make the last sentence end on the next page—this practically FORCES the reader to go on, just because of the human need for closure. Even better, ask a question. Start to answer the question on the current page but finish the answer on the next page.

- **Sales letter length:** Generally, longer sales letters work better than short ones. Take as much space as you need to tell the whole story. If your sales copy "moves," and if you are offering great benefits to the reader, he'll devour your letter and want more.

CAUTION

Stay away from the "Hot Mailing List" circulars or advertisements that you see in mail-order publications. Many of these lists aren't worth the match it would take to burn them.

- **No fancy stuff:** You want this to be a LETTER, not a sales pitch. As such, don't justify your margins, don't use lots of color and glossy pictures. Use the Courier type face—this makes it look more like a personally typewritten letter. Use black ink on white paper. Talk in a conversational tone, like you were sitting out on the front porch talking with a friend. Don't worry about grammar, just write like you talk. This is not a formal dissertation, it is a friendly, helpful letter to a friend.

- **Envelope:** Use a white or off-white envelope, and DON'T have your company logo on it. Just have your return address (no name, just the address lines) in black ink. This piques the recipients curiosity, rather than immediately giving your piece away as junk mail.

- **Ordering coupon:** Don't build the coupon into your sales letter. Use a separate piece of paper for your coupon. Some experts say the color you use makes a difference, others say it doesn't—so what are you going to do? Test of course (bet you knew that). The coupon should summarize the benefits the person is getting, but don't try to resell them on the coupon—doing so gives them cause to pause and reevaluate the offer.

> E-Z TIP
>
> For best response, hand-address or type the prospect's address on the envelope—or hire someone else to do it—handwritten addresses significantly increase the percentage of people who will open the envelope!

Remember, these are only rules of thumb, subject to change if your testing proves that other methods work better. The above tips represent several of the generally accepted rules for sales letters, but there is much more you should know before putting together your first test mailing. Look up some of the books in the Reference/Resources Section and read about the subject. There is no way the information contained in this section of this guide is going to tell you everything you need to know about direct mail marketing. It is up to you to avail yourself of the resources around you.

While the nature of direct mail precludes it from making use of some of the tools described in Chapter Two, many of them CAN be used and with far less cost than in the past thanks to new technology.

Your prospects should be able to place their order 24 hours a day by phone, FAX, e-mail, or through a web site, and all of these services are available at extremely low cost to you. If they want more information than you provide in your sales letter, you can make it available to them through autoresponder, fax-on-demand, or your web site.

note

Unfortunately, there is no magic formula that works in all cases, for every product or service and every market segment. You need to find the right "formula" for your marketing by constantly testing!

If they have more questions, they can e-mail you. You can have the answer to them within hours, or in some cases even minutes! When they see they are dealing with a real person, when they see they can get answers, they are more trusting. For less than $70/month (and the cost is going down all the time), you can provide all of these communications options to your customers:

- toll free order line (toll charges cost extra)
- 24-hour multi-line dedicated FAX
- fax-on-demand
- voice mail
- e-mail
- autoresponder
- Web site

If you handle their inquiries and orders correctly, you will have a great reputation for fast and customer-oriented service—and that could even become part of your USP!

Your Internet presence

Consider a retail store. Some of the business activities related to the store that you might observe (both on and off store property) on any given day are:

- sales
- samples
- advertising
- marketing tests
- customer surveys
- customer trend analysis
- customer data capture (address, phone, etc.)

Each of these business activities can be done on the Internet. Your web site is your storefront. Activities outside of your web site (see the next section on web site promotion) bring people to your "store" and activities inside your web site keep them coming back for more.

Let's consider each of the above activities.

Sales

Every product/service you offer can be part of your order form, or perhaps you want separate order forms for some of your higher priced items. And, your sales don't all have to originate at your storefront—sending e-mail to your previous customers or to opt-in or joint venture e-mail lists can also generate sales and increased store traffic.

Samples

As discussed, you can give out free reports, free subscriptions, or demo software. The beauty of this is that if you are giving away something in electronic form, it costs you nothing to deliver.

Advertising

E-Z TIP: In addition to online orders, your customers should have options for placing orders by phone and FAX.

This is pretty obvious. Your whole web site should be filled with sales messages that show your customers how your product or service solve their problem or give them what they want. In addition, your e-mail messages, e-zine classifieds and newsgroup messages (sig files) direct people to visit a particular section of your web site (store) for a special offer, or to an autoresponder message.

Marketing tests

Through the use of custom scripts, you can do "split-run" testing on your web site. If you have a link to a page about widgets, and you want to test the sale of widgets at different price levels, have that link send one person to a page where the widget is advertised for $7, send the next person to a page where it is advertised for $10, and send the next person to a page where the widget is $15. You can also test headlines, offers, bonuses or any other aspect of your sales message. Compare the "closing percentage" of the different pages and you'll quickly see which one sells best!

When you place advertisements in e-zines, you should have a way of "keying" those ads. One way of doing this is to have each advertisement send the reader to a different page on your website—a page made just for the readers of that ad. This way, when you count the number of times that page was accessed, you know how successful that particular advertisement was, and this helps you when it's time to decide where to place your future advertising.

Customer surveys/customer trend analysis

Interactive forms allow you to find out what is most important to your customers and prospects—what they really want, what problems they have, what they feel comfortable spending, what industry they come from, what advertising mediums they use most, and a myriad of other important information.

Customer data capture

When people sign up for a free newsletter or for your in-house mailing list (to be notified of any changes you make), capture as much contact information as you can. A minimum is their e-mail address, you would do well to capture their "snail-mail" information as well, and use it in your direct mail efforts.

> *note*
>
> If you give the customer what they ask for, they'll buy it and bless your name for selling it to them!

Getting customer feedback should be one of your top priorities, as customer input can have a significant impact on the direction you take in your future offerings and operations.

If you want to integrate the Internet into your marketing efforts, you need a minimum of three things: an e-mail address, an autoresponder, and a web site. There is no excuse not to have at least these tools—especially when there are companies who provide these tools FREE! In this chapter, I discuss various ways you can market on the Internet by using these tools as well as some of the other tools mentioned in Chapter Two.

Now, it is possible that you don't want to market on the Internet. Perhaps you just want to use the Internet as a way to improve your customer service—that by itself can be very valuable. But, keep your options open. If you are using direct marketing in any way, you can probably make good use of these Internet marketing methods.

Making your Web site a great place to visit . . . again and again!

Getting people to come to your web site is half the battle. Once they visit, they are just a mouse-click away from leaving at any time, so you better give them something worth staying for!

Your e-zine advertisements and SIG file should emphasize a benefit to be obtained by visiting your web site. This benefit could be any of the following:

1) Free reports—"Over 1300 Money-Making and Money Saving Reports You can Read Online Now!" (sound familiar?)

2) Free Book—"Get a free health/fitness book just for visiting!"

3) Free subscription—"Get a 1 year subscription to *Smart Shopper* now!"

4) Free software—"Come get your free home maintenance 'how to' software now!"

5) Contest/Drawing—"Enter to win a new computer!"

6) Information—"Learn how you can save 35% off your grocery bills"

7) News—"Daily Updates on Women Issues Legislation"

Obviously, there are more ways to interest people in your site than those listed above. Generally, you should offer them something of value free of charge. That doesn't mean you have to incur an expense giving it to them, heck no! You can have valuable information on your site that they can read, or you can offer a weekly/monthly e-zine or online newsletter.

Once they come by, your site should offer an abundance of information related to the stated benefit. For instance, I would think that on a site where you used "Win a New Computer!" as your hook to get the visitor, you would offer information about computers such as:

- How to Get the Best Price on a New Computer
- How to Upgrade Your Current Computer and Save Hundreds of Dollars
- How to Buy Used Computers Without Getting Ripped Off
- Should You or Should You NOT Purchase an Extended Warranty on Your Computer?
- How to Get the Most Money from Your Used Computer
- Which Upgrades will Increase Your Computer Performance the Most?

Naturally, you plug your own company products/services related to buying, selling, and upgrading new and used computers and computer upgrade equipment. Each of the above articles might briefly describe why your company is uniquely positioned to serve the visitor's computer upgrade needs better than anyone else, and act as an invitation to read more about how you can solve their problems.

Make it fast

When designing your web site, there is one technical aspect that has a significant impact on the success of your site: download speed. There are a few well known rules for designing a quick-loading web page. They are:

- the fewer graphics (pictures) the better (but you should have a few)
- don't use large tables

- when you DO use graphics:
  - ✦ always use height/width tags. This way your visitor can read the text on your web page while waiting for the graphics to load.
  - ✦ use smallest number of colors necessary (and use standard 216 color palette)
  - ✦ use GIF file format (instead of JPEG) except for scanned pictures

If you aren't familiar with some of the terms in the above list, don't worry. I listed some web sites and software programs in the References/Resources Chapter to help you learn about web site design. Any internet consultant or professional web page designer should be well acquainted with these terms as well.

CAUTION If it takes any longer than 10 seconds to load your page, many people will leave before they get a chance to read the first sentence!

When designing your web page, remember your ultimate goal: *to make sales.* Your goal is NOT to receive the "Cool Web Site" award. Your goal is NOT to be recognized in the web-design community for your brilliant implementation of streaming video, Java applets, or digital sound. While they are neat, they take way too much time to download with the typical dial-up connection.

Leave these things to the people who design web pages as an artistic or creative outlet. Concentrate your efforts on keeping your target audience at your website long enough to capture their attention and interest, and leading them to an inquiry or direct sale.

note If you don't want to learn HTML, you don't have to! There are programs (see the resource section for details) that allow you to create a web page simply by dragging and dropping text and pictures onto a work area—then they generate the HTML code for you. Create a few pages like this, link them together, and you have your site. Your web site doesn't need to start out with 100 pages . . . start out with 5 to 10 and add new pages as you need them.

> *note* Don't let the idea of creating your own web site scare you. With the new software tools, it's almost as easy as typing a letter.

Get 'em to come back

Getting people to return to your site after the initial visit may be the biggest challenge to operating a web site, and it should be a very important part of you online strategy. The more often they are exposed to your site (and the sales messages) the more chance of getting a sale.

Update your site regularly; don't let it get stale. Add new content, or update the content you have. If you have a monthly contest running, change the award from month to month. If you offer an e-zine, tell people about any changes you made at your website. Even if you don't have an e-zine, you should be doing something to capture visitors' e-mail addresses and sending out an announcement when you make any significant changes to your site.

One very effective way to keep people coming back on a regular basis is to host your own online discussion group (see Chapter Two). I highly recommend this tool to anyone with a website. Other possibilities for getting regular traffic is a classified ads section, or a weekly drawing for free stuff. That's a good way to get e-mail addresses too.

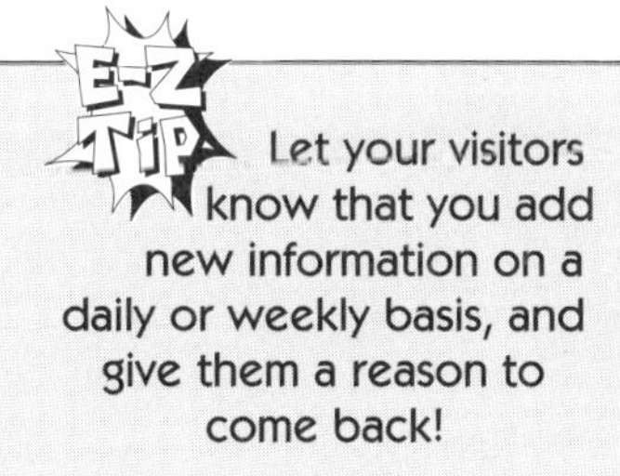

Keep it interesting; like a real store, your web site should be dynamic. You should add new products that your research showed to have sales potential, and dropping the slow sellers. Change your offers frequently, change your promotions from time to time. Change the look of your site every once in a while. A real store doesn't keep up the same signs and run the same advertising week after week, and neither should yours.

Web site promotion: getting the word out

The first thing you need to do after you get your own website is to let people know it's there. There are many ways to get the word out and you should use them all.

Search engines

Once you have your web site up and running, the first thing you need to do is get it listed in the online search engines and directories. Some of the most popular of these are:

Alta Vista	Lycos
Excite	Webcrawler
Hotbot	Yahoo!
InfoSeek	

Your "drop-in" traffic comes from being listed in the above web resources. By *drop-in* I mean people that come looking for something you offer, rather than you advertising to them. When people go to the search engines and directories, they have a specific item or service they are looking for—somewhat like the yellow pages. Think of your web page title as your HEADLINE. Spend the time required to get it right (go back and reread the discussion on headlines).

On this and the next two pages, I reproduced an article about successful search engine submissions written by Greg Landry. Besides containing must have information about getting a good listing on the various search engines, this is an excellent example of using an article as free advertising—note the resource box at the end of the article.

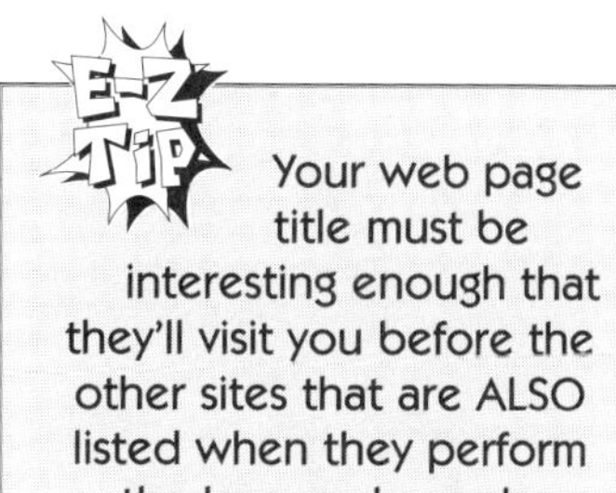

The Search Engine "Dilemma"...Fact and Fiction

13 Keys To Listing Your Web Site For Highest Possible Placement!

by Greg Landry, M.S.

If you've been on the 'net for any period of time, I'm sure you've heard a lot of talk about listing a web site on search engines(data bases of web sites that can be searched by keyword(s) or in some cases category). Good placement on search engines is critical to your online marketing efforts!

Although I've done considerable research in this area, I certainly don't claim to know it all and I'm very open to your comments/suggestions on this subject.... Greg@Landry.com

Here are 13 keys to improving your placement on search engines.

1. When submitting your web site, keep in mind that there are essentially two types of search engines. Robot engines send a "robot" to your site to capture and catalog all the info on your site. These include WebCrawler, Excite, Lycos, Alta Vista, Infoseek, Hotbot, and Inktomi. The second type only uses the info that you give it. These include Yahoo!, www Yellow Pages, EINet Galaxy, Open Text, WWW Worm, and World Wide Yellow Pages.

2. For best results, always submit your information to each search engine individually rather than using a submission service. It's important to be able to tailor your info for each specific search engine. It takes more time but is well worth it.

3. Brainstorm for a list of 30 or 40 keywords (or combinations of words "horse stables") for your site. Then, number the keywords based on what your prospective customer would most likely be using as a keyword. Although you need a strong list of about 20, your first 5 or so are critical.

4. Use the plural when possible. If you list your keyword as "horse stable," but someone searches for "horse stables," it will not find your site. However, if you list your keyword as "horse stables" and someone searches for "horse stable," it pulls up your site!

5. The title of your site is **VERY** important! Your title is NOT the first headline on your page, but rather what appears on the title bar of your browser (upper left part of page in Netscape). Most search engines treat the words in your title as MAJOR keywords. Carefully choose two or three keywords to put in your title, but keep in mind that it should not just be a list of keywords. It should make sense. Also, if you make it too long, it will be cut-off. The search engines weigh the importance of a word in your title based on density. For example, if you have five words in your title and one of them is horse, then it will comprise 20% of your title. But, if you only have two words in your title and one of them is horse, then it comprises 50% of your title and is "weighed" much more heavily as a keyword!

6. Use your keywords FREQUENTLY in your text at the VERY BEGINNING of your web site. Try not to put tables, graphics or anything else at the top of your site. It should just be text that is rich with your major keywords. Here again, just as in the title, the search engines look at the DENSITY of your keywords rather just the number of keywords. Also, keep in mind that you're NOT just listing keywords here. This is actually the text of your web site.

7. "Meta tags" are NOT a magic formula for getting listed at the top of search engines, but they may help on Alta Vista, Hotbot, and Infoseek. A meta tag, for our purposes, is a way of providing a description and keywords that are only visible to the robots from the search engines. However, there is debate over how much weight these are given. The meta tags must go *inside* the header tags, so it looks like this:

```
<HEAD>
<TITLE>your title here</TITLE>
<META name="description" content="your site description goes here">
<META name="keywords" content="your keywords go here">
</HEAD>
```

8. DON'T "keyword" spam! This is a practice that many used for good search engine placement, but it's considered bad etiquette and the search engines are all starting to penalize you when they catch it! It's done by repeating keywords *numerous* times either in the meta tag or within the text of the page, sometimes where it can't be seen unless you go to the HTML. I think this is a waste of time and will eventually backfire on you. Just try to legitimately use your keywords as much as you can in the initial paragraphs of text on your web site.

9. Be sure that your site is COMPLETELY ready and online before you list your site with any search engines.

10. Your title beginning with a letter that's low in the alphabet (abcd) may help in some of the standard search engines such as Yahoo!, but it's really hard to tell how much that comes into play. I certainly would NOT change my site title to something like "AAA horses" just for the sake of starting with an "a." If you can legitimately start your title with a,b,c,d, etc., great, otherwise don't worry about it.

11. Before you list with each search engine, put in your top three or four keywords, and see what comes up. Go to the first few sites that are listed. Once the web site has completely transferred to your computer, click on "view" and then on "document source." This will show you the HTML for that web site. What's unique about this site that caused it to be listed first with this search engine? Does the title contain the keywords? Are keywords used frequently in the text? Are keywords listed in meta tags? etc. Now look at the second and third sites listed. Are they unique in the same way as the first one? What do they have in common? This gives you a good idea of what "ranks" with this search engine.

12. If you're marketing online, many people believe that OVER 50% of your hits will come from Yahoo! It's probably worth spending a considerable amount of your time trying to get good placement on this search engine.

13. Be patient. Many search engines take weeks to get you in the system.

Greg Landry publishes a free e-mail newsletter . . .
"HomeBased and Online"! To start your subscription,
e-mail Homebased@Landry.com or call or fax Greg . . .
Ph. 504-766-1004 Fax 504-766-1014

Besides listing your site with these major resources, there are many other Internet directory and index sites that you can list your site on at no cost. So many, in fact, that you could literally spend days or even weeks trying to find them all and fill out their list forms.

Fortunately, there are some tools that make this job easier. There are web sites that allow you to submit your web site listing to several places at once. There is also software available that allows you to do this on your own. Contact information for both of these options is available in the References/Resources Chapter.

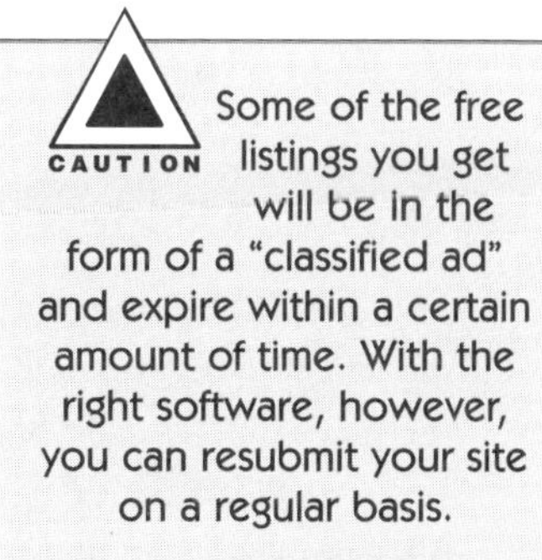

Using the software allows you to pick and choose which directories/indices you will submit your site to. There may be some you don't want to submit to. For instance, if you manually submitted a specific "tuned for a given search engine" web page to all the major resources, you wouldn't want to resubmit your listing via the automated methods, because that would probably give you a lower ranking. So, using the software you could exclude the places your site was already listed.

E-zine, e-mail list, newsgroup and discussion group advertising

Search engines give you drop-in traffic, but you shouldn't stop there. If there are e-zines or e-mail lists that are related to your product or service, place classified ads there (if they accept advertising, of course). The cost of advertising in these publications is very small. You might want to make several copies of your web site home page (the *home page* of your web site is just the first page) and link different e-zine ads to different copies. That way, you can track the results of your e-zine advertising.

DEFINITION

Remember the Greg Landry search engine report included earlier in this chapter? You could submit similar reports (related to your area of expertise) to some of these online forums too. As long as you provide useful, topical information, your report will be appreciated by the others in the forum. Be sure to include your own contact information or resource box in the report for those who want more information.

Instead of linking your classified and SIG messages to your web site, you may want to link them to your autoresponder—or why not both? This way the prospect may choose whatever method they prefer to get your information. You can also include a voice mail phone number and/or a fax-on-demand number. Test it out and see how/if it works.

Opt-in e-mail

Remember, opt-in e-mail means that all the people on the list requested information related to the list topic. Your cost to send an e-mail to these folks is 10 to 25 cents. So, even though it's not free, it does cost considerably less than a conventional direct mail campaign. One big difference between direct e-mail and direct (conventional) mail is the length of the message. Your e-mail message should be relatively short. Don't try to sell anything. All you want to do is get them to request a document from your autoresponder, or visit your website. Once they take that step, you have the room you need to show them all the benefits of your offer.

News bureaus

For $225 (as of December, 1997) the "Internet News Bureau" sends an e-mail press release about your site to 1,200 online media outlets. Or, for only $55 they send a site announcement to these same 1,200 media outlets. If your site is newsworthy, this might be a very good investment! By newsworthy, I mean if you're offering something new or unusual, or demonstrably better than similar items. Check them out in the Reference/Resource Chapter.

Offline promotion

Right along with your address and phone number, you should have your Internet contact information on everything bearing your company name. That

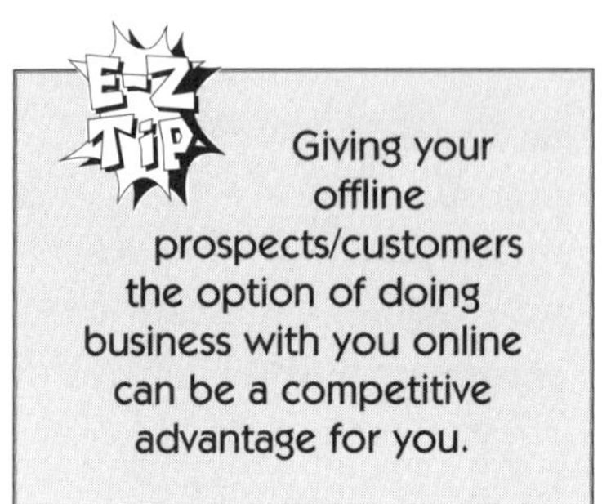

means envelopes, letterheads, business cards, sales letters, packing slips, shipping labels, everything.

Even if you don't get more sales directly, the improved customer service that is possible with the Internet tools could translate to better customer satisfaction and, indirectly, more orders.

Resources and reference material

4

Chapter 4

Resources and reference material

What you'll find in this chapter:

- Marketing books
- Data service publications
- High-volume ad placement
- Services that can help your business
- Internet sites and services

This chapter was arranged so that it roughly corresponds with the order of the first three chapters. For instance, copywriting was discussed earlier in this guide (Chapter One), so reference books about copywriting are one of the first things you find listed in this chapter. Internet marketing tools are listed towards the end of this chapter, since they were discussed later.

Books for the direct marketing library

I compiled a list of books you should study if you want to be successful in direct marketing. As I began this compilation, I quickly realized that a listing and description of every good book on the subject would require a book itself.

This being the case, I can't claim the below list to be comprehensive. There are many other books you would do well to acquaint yourself with, but this is a very, VERY good start, and anyone that reads and applies the knowledge contained in these books will do very well indeed.

Even though it's not a comprehensive list, it is pretty long, so don't let that scare you. You don't have to read every one of these books before you do anything. As I mentioned earlier, there are some people that study themselves right out of business—spending thousands of dollars and hundreds of hours studying books, manuals and courses, listening to cassette tapes and watching videos, attending seminars. But, THEY NEVER DO ANYTHING. Don't be one of those people. Study a few books and then DO something . . . you'll learn volumes of information from the results you get after taking action. Dreaming is good, but DOING is what makes dreams happen—be a DOER!

I separated the books into different categories. The first category is "General Direct Marketing"—which in this case means books that aren't specifically about copywriting or internet marketing—the topics of the next two sections.

Many of these books can be found at your local library, others you will have to purchase. Eventually you'll want your own copies anyway, so you can refer to them often and make notes in the margins. I included web site addresses where you can read more about the most of these books and even order them if you desire. I only wish all the books could be ordered from MY website. That would be a nice feather in my cap, let me tell you!

Speaking of web site addresses, you'll note that some of them are for the Amazon online bookstore. You would do well to just visit that site and browse around for awhile. You could spend hours there finding all kinds of fascinating and useful information that will aid in your success.

The titles marked with an asterisk (*) are also featured in the "special offer" at the end of this guide.

GENERAL DIRECT MARKETING BOOKS

Direct-Mail & Direct Response Advertising Techniques the "Experts" Don't Want You to Know About!*
by T.E. Mudry
Web site address: http://www.palis.com/p0000125.htm

How-To Advertise and Get Maximum & Immediate Sales From Your Ad!*
by T.E. Mudry
Web site address: http://www.palis.com/p0000124.htm

Your Own "Kitchen-Table" Business for Under $200!*
by T.E. Mudry
Web site address: http://www.palis.com/p0000123.htm

Making Money With Classified Ads
by Melvin Powers
Web site address: http://www.mpowers.com/bmp.htm

How to Get Rich in Mail Order
by Melvin Powers
Web site address: http://www.mpowers.com/bmp.htm

A Lifetime of Homework
by George W. Haylings

Marketing Without a Marketing Budget
by Craig S. Rice
Web site address: http://www.magic7.com/htg/browse.html

How To Market a Product For Under $500!
by Jeffrey Dobkin
Web site address: http://www.magic7.com/htg/browse.html

INTERNET MARKETING BOOKS

Web Wealth
by Jeffrey Lant

Insider Internet Marketing
by Jim Daniels

The Amazing Formula
by Marlon Sanders
http://www.higherresponse.com/track/t.cgi/8338

Cyber Wealth
by George Kosch & Sandi Hunter
http://www.incor.com/inc_cybr.htm

eMarketing
by Seth Godin
Web site address: http://www.amazon.com

Online Marketing Handbook
Daniel S. Janal
Web site address: http://www.amazon.com

Web Advertising and Marketing
by Paul J. Dowlings Jr., Thomas J. Kuegler Jr., and Joshua O. Testerman
Web Site address: http://www.amazon.com

COPYWRITING BOOKS

Cash Copy
by Jeffrey Lant

Magic Words That Bring You Riches
Ted Nicholas

Direct Mail Copy that Sells
by Herschell Gordon Lewis
Web site address: http://www.amazon.com

The Ultimate Sales Letter
by Daniel S. Kennedy

Words that Sell
by Richard Bayan
Web site address: http://www.amazon.com

These next several books on copywriting are "classics" on the subject, authored by some of the pioneers in the field. The referred website is Carl Galletti's "*Hard to Get Books and Tapes*" site—I urge you to visit this site, it will be well worth your time. Hang on to your wallet when you get there—Carl's own copywriting could make you happily part with a few thousand bucks. You were warned! You may also be able to find some of these books on the Amazon site (www.amazon.com), and of course they should also be in your local library.

My Life in Advertising/ Scientific Advertising
by Claude Hopkins
Web site address: http://www.magic7.com/htg/

The Lasker Story as He Told It
by Albert Lasker
Web site address: http://www.magic7.com/htg/

The First Hundred Million
by E. Haldeman-Julius
Web site address: http://www.magic7.com/htg/

How to Make Your Advertising Make Money
by John Caples
Web site address: http://www.magic7.com/htg/

How to Write a Good Advertisement!—A Short Course in Copywriting
by Vic Schwab
Web site address: http://www.magic7.com/htg/

How To Make Maximum Money in Minimum Time: 16 Of The Fastest Cash-Producing Secrets Known To Man!
by Gary C. Halbert
Web site address: http://www.magic7.com/htg/

Ogilvy on Advertising
by David Ogilvy
Web site address: http://www.magic7.com/htg/

Reason Why Advertising Plus Intensive Advertising
by John E. Kennedy/Lord & Thomas
Web site address: http://www.magic7.com/htg/

Tested Advertising Methods
by John Caples
Web site address: http://www.magic7.com/htg/

POWER WORDS

Here are some "emotional" words that will help get your copy read.

1. Absolutely
2. Advice to
3. Amazing
4. Announcing
5. Approved
6. At last
7. Attractive
8. Authentic
9. Bargain
10. Beautiful
11. Better
12. Big
13. Breakthrough
14. Colorful
15. Colossal
16. Complete
17. Confidential
18. Crammed
19. Delivered
20. Direct
21. Discount
22. Discover
23. Do you
24. Easily
25. Endorsed
26. Enormous
27. Excellent
28. Exciting
29. Exclusive
30. Expert
31. Famous
32. Fascinating
33. Fortune
34. Free
35. Full
36. Genuine
37. Gift
38. Gigantic
39. Greatest
40. Guaranteed
41. Hate
42. Helpful
43. Here
44. Highest
45. How
46. How to
47. Huge
48. Immediately
49. Improved
50. Informative
51. Instructive
52. Interesting
53. Largest
54. Latest
55. Lavishly
56. Liberal
57. Life
58. Lifetime
59. Limited
60. Love
61. Lowest
62. Magic
63. Mammoth
64. Miracle
65. New
66. Noted
67. Now
68. Odd
69. Only
70. Outstanding
71. Personalized
72. Popular
73. Powerful
74. Practical
75. Professional
76. Profitable
77. Profusely
78. Protect
79. Proven
80. Quality
81. Quickly

82. Rare
83. Reduced
84. Refundable
85. Remarkable
86. Reliable
87. Revealing
88. Revolutionary
89. Sale
90. Scarce
91. Secrets
92. Security
93. Selected
94. Sensational
95. Simplified
96. Sizable
97. Special
98. Startling
99. Strange
100. Strong
101. Sturdy
102. Successful
103. Superior
104. Surprise
105. Terrific
106. Tested
107. Tremendous
108. Unconditional
109. Unique
110. Unlimited
111. Unparalleled
112. Unsurpassed
113. Unusual
114. Useful
115. Valuable
116. Wealth
117. Weird
118. Wonderful
119. Yes
120. You

Standard Rate and Data Service Publications

Standard Rate and Data Service (SRDS) publications are "must use" resources for the direct response marketer. They are *the* source for advertising media data, and all the professional advertising agencies subscribe to their service. A subscription to one of their publications can be several hundred dollars (depending on which publication you subscribe to) but they can also be found at most large public libraries. You may also be able to get an acquaintance in an advertising firm to give you their old copy when they get their new one (new issues come out several times a year). The SRDS publications of most interest are:

1. **Consumer Magazines Advertising Source:** Listings for over 3,000 consumer magazines and card decks, including over 300 international magazines.

2. **Business Publications Advertising Source:** Listings for over 8,500 business publications including over 1,200 international publications.

For each magazine or publication listed in the above two resources, you are given the following information:

- Publisher's Editorial Profile
- Personnel
- Representatives/Branch Offices
- Commission and Cash Discount
- General Rate Policy
- Black/White Rates
- Color Rates
- Covers
- Inserts
- Bleed
- Special Position
- Classified Mail Order/Specialty Rates
- Split-run
- Special Issue Rates and Data
- Geographic and/or Demographic Editions
- Contract and Copy Regulations
- General Requirements
- Issue and Closing Dates
- Special Services
- Circulation

3. **Direct Marketing List Source:** This BIBLE of mailing lists is immense, containing over 19,000 listings in 212 categories—including coops and package insert programs. I highly recommend that you go to your library and just spend a few hours going through the pages of this fantastic resource. It's an excellent "idea generator" for your own marketing.

See how many lists there are related to your product/service. Perhaps you can adapt your product for national sales and distribution through the mail. You'll be surprised by the number of ideas you get just by going through this gem. Plan on investing a MINIMUM of 2-3 hours just looking through the various listings.

For each list, you are given the following information:

Personnel	Description
List Source	Commission
Method of Addressing	Delivery Schedule
Restrictions	Fields of Specialization
Selections Available	Fees and Deposits
Mail Services	Test Arrangement
Letter Shop Services	Quantity and Rental Rates

The SRDS also has a publication titled *Newspapers Advertising Source* which contains over 3,200 listings of newspapers. Each listing includes the following information:

- Newspaper buying reference material
- Market data by census region and by state, including population, households, effective buying income (EBI) and retail sales
- SAU (Standard Advertising Unit) definitions
- Newspaper representatives section, including newspaper groups and rep firms
- National newspaper listings
- Daily newspapers by state
- National newspaper classified rates and data
- Daily newspaper classified rates and data by state
- International newspapers
- Newspaper comics and newspaper distributed magazines
- Weeklies and specialized newspapers
- College and university newspapers
- Black newspapers

On the following pages are the list of classifications for the Direct Mail Lists and for the Consumer Magazines Advertising Source and Business Publications Advertising Source. Just looking through the classifications may be enough to give you ideas about your future marketing.

SRDS Direct Mail List Classifications

BUSINESS LISTS

Advertising & Marketing
Air Conditioning, Plumbing & Heating, Sheet Metal & Ventilating
Amusements
Appliances
Architecture
Arts
Automating Data
Processing-Computers
Automotive, Automobiles,Tires,
Batteries, Accessories
Service Stations, Garages
Aviation & Aerospace
Baking
Banking & Financial
Barbers
Beauty & Hairdressing
Boating
Books & Book Trade
Bottling
Building Management & Real Estate
Business Executives
Business Firms
Campus & Camping
Cemetery, Monument & Funeral Supplies
Ceramic
Certified Public Accounting
Chain Stores
Chemical & Chemical Process Industries
Clothing & Furnishing Goods (Men's)
Clothing & Furnishing Goods (Women's)
Coal Merchandising
Coin-operated & Vending
Machines
Confectionery
Control & Instrumentation Systems
Corsets, Brassieres & Undergarments
Cosmetics
Dairy Products
Dental
Department, general
Merchandise & Specialty Stores
Discount Marketing
Display
Drugs, Pharmaceutics
Educational
Electrical
Electronic Engineering
Engineering & Construction
Engineers
Farm Implements & Supplies
Feed, Grain & Milling
Fertilizer &Agricultural Chemicals
Fire Protection
Fishing Commercial
Floor Coverings
Florists and Floriculture
Food Processing &
Distribution
Nursing & Health
Ocean Science & Engineering
Funeral Directors
Fur Trade, Farming,Trapping, etc.
Furniture & Upholstery
Gas
Giftware, Antiques, Art Goods, Decorative Accessories, Greeting Cards, etc.
Glass
Golf
Government Administrative Services
Services & Public Works, Municipal Township, County, State, Federal
Grocery
Hardware & Housewares
Home Economics
Home Furnishings
Hospital & Hospital
Administration Hotels, Motels, Club & Resorts
Human Resources
Industrial Distribution
Industrial Purchasing
Infant's, Children's & Teenage Goods
Institutions
Insurance
Interior Design/Space
Planning
International Trade
Jewelry & Watchmaking
Journalism
Landscape, Garden Supplies, Seed & Nursery Trade
Laundry & Dry Cleaning
Leather, Boots & Shoes
Legal
Lighting & Lighting Fixtures
Lumber & Forest Industries
Maintenance
Materials Handling & Distribution
Meats & Provisions
Medical & Surgical
Metal, Metalworking & Machinery
Mining (Coal, Metal & Nonmetallic)
Motion, Talk, Sound, Commercial Pictures, etc.
Trucks & Accessories
Motorcycle & Bicycle
Moving & Storage
Music & Music Trades
Office Equipment & Stationery
Office Equipment Mail Order
Buyers
Office Methods & Management
Optical & Optometry
Packaging (Mfrs.) & Paperboard Packaging (Users)
Paint, Painting & Decorating
Paper Parks, Public
Petroleum & Oil
Pets & Pet Supplies
Photographic
Plant & Manufacturing Executives
Plastics & Composition
Products
Police Detective & Security
Pollution Control, Environment,
Energy
Power & Power Plants
Printing & Printing
Processes
Produce (Fruits & Vegetables)
Product Design
Engineering
Public Transportation
Radio & Television
Railroad
Religious
Rental & Leasing
Equipment
Restaurants & Food Service
Roads, Streets, etc.
Roofing
Rubber
Safety, Accident Prevention
Sales Management
Schools & School Administration
Science, Research & Development
Selling & Salesmanship
Sporting Goods
Stone Products, etc.
Swimming Pools
Telephone & Communications
Textiles & Knit Goods
Toys, Hobbies & Novelties
Trailers & Accessories
Transportation, Shipping & Shipping Room Supplies
Travel
Veterinary
Water Supply & Sewage Disposal
Welding
Wire & Wire Products
Woodworking

CONSUMER LISTS

Almanacs & Directories
Art & Antiques
Automotive
Aviation
Babies
Boating & Yachting
Brides
Business Leaders
Children's
Collectibles
College & Alumni
Contributors (Philanthropic)
Crafts, Hobbies & Models
Credit Card Holders
Disabilities
Dogs & Pets
Dressmaking & Needlework
Education & Self Improvement
Entertainment
Epicurean & Specialty Foods
Ethnic Fashions - Clothing
Fishing & Hunting
Fraternal, Professional
Groups, Service Clubs & Associates
Game Buyers, Contest Participants
Gardening (Home)
Gay & Lesbian
General
General Merch. Mail Order Buyers
Gifts - Gift Buyers
Health
Home & Family Service
Horses, Riding & Breeding
Insurance Buyers
Investors
Labor - Trade Unions
Land Investors
Literature & Book Buyers
Mechanics & Science
Men's
Military, Naval & Veterans
Music & Record Buyers
Occult, Astrological & Metaphysical
Occupant & Resident
Opportunity Seekers
Photography
Political & Social Topics
Premium & Catalog Buyers
Professional
Religious & Denominational
Senior Citizens
Society
Sports
Teenagers
Travel
Video & Home Computers
Women's

FARM LISTS

Dairy & Dairy Breeds
Diversified Farming & Farm Home
Farm Education & Vocations
Field Crops & Soil Management
Livestock & Breed
Poultry

SRDS Consumer Magazine Classifications

Affluence
Airline Inflight/Train Enroute
Almanacs & Directories
Art and Antiques
Automotive
Aviation
Babies
Black/African American
Boating and Yachting
Bridal
Business & Finance
Campers, Recreational Vehicles, Motor Homes & Trailers
Camping & Outdoor Recreation
Children's
Civic
College and Alumni
Comics & Comic Technique
Computers
Crafts, Games, Hobbies & Models
Dancing
Disabilities
Dogs & Pets
Dressmaking & Needlework
Editorialized & Classified Advertising
Education & Teacher
Entertainment Guides & Programs
Entertainment and Performing Arts
Epicurean
Fashion, Beauty & Grooming
Fishing & Hunting
Fitness
Fraternal, Professional Groups, Service Clubs, Veteran's Organizations & Associations
Gaming
Gardening (Home)
Gay Publications
General Editorial
Group Buying Opportunities
Health
History
Home Service & Home
Horses, Riding & Breeding
Hotel In-room
Labor, Trade Union
Literary, Book Reviews & Writing Techniques
Mechanics & Science
Media/Personalities
Men's
Metropolitan/Regional/State
Metropolitan/Entertainment, Radio & TV
Military & Naval (Air Force, Army, Navy & Marines)
Motorcycle
Music
Mystery, Adventure & Science Fiction
Nature & Ecology
News-Weeklies
News-Biweeklies, Dailies, Semimonthlies
Newsweeklies (Alternatives)
Newsletters
Newspaper Distributed Magazines
Parenthood
Photography
Political & Social Topics
Religious & Denominational
Science/Technology
Sex
Special Interest Publications
Sports
Teen
Travel
TV, Radio/Communications & Electronics
Women's
Youth

SRDS Business Publications Classifications

Advertising & Marketing
Air Conditioning, Heating, Plumbing, Refrigeration Sheet Metal & Ventilating
Amusements & Gaming Management
Appliances
Architecture
Arts
Automotive, Automobiles, Tires, Batteries, Accessories, Service Stations, Garages
Aviation & Aerospace
Baking
Banking
Beauty & Hairdressing
Boating
Books & Book Trade
Bottling
Brewing, Distilling & Beverages
Brick, Tile Building Materials
Brushes, Brooms & Mops
Building
Building Management & Real Estate
Building Products Retailing
Business
Business-Metro, State & Regional
Campgrounds, Recreational Camps
Cemetery & Monuments
Ceramics
Chain stores
Chemical & Chemical Process Industries
China & Dinnerware
Clothing & Furnishing Goods (Men's)
Clothing & Furnishing Goods (Women's)
Coin-Operated & Vending Machines
Computers
Confectionery
Control & Instrumentation Systems
Cosmetics
Dairy Products (Milk, Ice Cream, Milk Products)
Department Specialty Stores
Discount Marketing
Display
Draperies & Curtains
Educational
Educational, Adult Training, Motivation & Development
Electrical
Electronic Engineering
Electronic Imaging
Employment Opportunities & Recruitment
Energy Application & Management
Engineering & Construction
Farm Implements (general)
Farm Supplies
Fashion Accessories
Feed, Grain & Milling
Fertilizer & Agricultural Chemicals
Financial
Fire Protection
Fishing, Commercial
Fitness Professional
Floor Coverings
Florists & Floriculture
Food - Processing & Distribution
Fundraising/Philanthropy
Funeral Directors
Fur Farming
Furniture Upholstery
Gas
Giftware, Antiques, Art Goods, Decorative Accessories, Greeting Cards, etc.
Glass
Golf
Government (Local, State & Federal) & Public Works
Graphic Design
Grocery
Hardware
Home Economics
Home Furnishings
Horse & Rider Supplies, Apparel, & Equipment
Hotels, Motels, Clubs & Resorts
Housewares
Human Resources
Industrial
Industrial Automation
Industrial Design
Industrial Distribution
Industrial Purchasing
Industrial Purchasing Directories & Catalogs
Infants, Children's & Teenage Goods
Insurance
Interior Design/Furnishings/ Space Planning
International Trade
Intimate Apparel
Jewelry & Watchmaking
Journalism & Publishing
Landscape, Garden Supplies
Laundry & Dry-Cleaning
Leather, Boots & Shoes
Legal
Lighting & Lighting Fixtures
Linens & Domestics
Logging & Forest Products Manufacturing
Market
Luggage & Leather Goods
Maintenance
Manufacturing/Industries, Equipment, Products & Systems
Maritime, Marine, Shipbuilding, Repair & Operating Materials
Materials Handling & Distribution
Meats & Provisions
Metal, Metalworking & Machinery
Military & Naval (Active & Inactive Service)
Mining (Coal, Metal & Non-Metallic)
Motion, Talk, Sound, Commercial Pictures, etc.
Motor Trucks & Accessories
Motorcycle & bicycle
Moving & Storage
Music & Music Trades
Newsletters
Nuclear Science & Engineering
Ocean Science & Engineering
Office Equipment & Stationery
Office Methods & Management
Oils (Vegetable)
Packaging Manufacturers (Including-Paperboard & Flexible Packaging)
Packaging (Users)
Paint & Wallcoverings, Painting & Decorating
Paper
Parks, Public
Petroleum & Oil
Pets
Photographic
Physical Distribution
Plant/Engineering, Maintenance, Repair & Operations
Plastics & Composition Products
Police, Law Enforcement & Penology
Pollution Control (Air & Water)
Poultry & Poultry Products
Power & Power Plants
Printing & Printing Processes
Produce (Fruits & Vegetables)
Product Design Engineering
Professional Association Management
Public Transportation & Mass Transit
Quality Assurance
Radio, TV & Video
Railroad
Religious
Rental & Leasing Equipment

Reproduction - Inplant & Commercial
Restaurants & Food Service
Robotics
Roofing
Rubber
Safety, Accident Prevention
Sales Management
School Administration
Science, Research & Development
Security
Seed & Nursery Trade
Selling & Salesmanship
Shopping Centers
Sporting Goods
Stone Products, etc.
Sugar & Sugar Crops
Swimming Pools
Tea, Coffee, Spices
Telecommunications Technology
Textiles & Knit Goods
Tobacco
Toys, Hobbies, Novelties
Trailers & Accessories
Transportation, Traffic, Shipping & Shipping Room Supplies
Travel, Business Conventions & Meetings
Travel, Retail
Veterinary
Waste Management
Water Supply & Sewage Disposal
Welding Wire & Wire Products
Woodworking

HEALTHCARE

Biotechnological Sciences
Dental
Drugs, Pharmaceutics
Healthcare
Hospital Administration
Medical & Surgical
Nursing & Health
Optical & Optometric

HIGH VOLUME AD PLACEMENT

Once you tested your classified or small display advertisement and found it to be successful, you can expand your testing to larger and larger groups. If you're going to submit an advertisement to many different publications, you will save yourself a lot of time and money by doing it through the companies listed below. They specialize in placing ads in multiple magazines and at a much discounted price.

National Mail Order Classified
(941) 366-3003

National Response Corporation
(954) 747-7584
FAX: (954) 749-2831

Quick Classified Advertising, Inc.
(800) 854-1841
FAX: (816) 627-0005

This company specializes in placing advertisements in statewide weekly/shopper publications networks (NOT the same papers as served by the state press associations).

State Press Associations also work with you to place advertisements in a network of many different newspapers—in your state as well as others. Contact information for these organizations is listed on the next page.

STATE CLASSIFIED ASSOCIATIONS

(This information was correct to the best of my knowledge when compiled, but is not guaranteed.)

State	Phone	Cost	Circulation	Min # Words	#Weekly or Biweekly papers / Total # papers
Alabama	205 871-7737	$165.00	880,000	25	96 / 117
Arizona	602 261-7655	$160.00	780,000	25	52 / 64
Arkansas	501 374-1500	$149.00	900,000	25	108 / 141
California	916 449-6000	$400.00	3,100,000	25	149 / 183
Colorado	303 571-5117	$150.00	540,000	25	86 / 102
Florida	904 222-5790	$250.00	1,660,000	25	84 / 95
Georgia	770 454-6776	$200.00	1,400,000	20	80 / 97
Idaho	208 375-0733	$125.00	325,000	25	37 / 41
Illinois	217 523-5096	$330.00	990,000	25	159 / 188
Indiana	317 637-3966	$225.00	1,200,000	25	??? / 107
Iowa	515 244-2145	$190.00	1,400,000	25	242 / 269
Kansas	913 271-5304	$180.00	500,000	25	86 / 118
Kentucky	502 223-8821	$179.00	1,000,000	25	17 / 67
Lousiana	504 344-9309	$200.00	800,000	25	??? / 94
MD DC DE	410 263-7878	$175.00	1,400,000	25	57 / 67
Michigan	517 372-2424	$239.00	1,400,000	25	82 / 107
Minnesota	612 332-8844	$199.00	2,000,000	25	263 / 280
Mississippi	601 981-3060	$150.00	1,500,000	25	78 / 96
Missouri	314 449-4167	$169.00	913,000	25	141 / 166
Montana	406 443-2850	$109.00	209,000	25	53 / 60
Nebraska	402 476-2851	$145.00	460,000	25	167 / 183
Nevada	702 885-0866	$ 99.00	370,000	25	??? / 23
New England[1]	617 373-5610	$250.00	1,260,000	25	157 / 165
New Jersey	609 406-0600	$279.00	1,800,000	25	103 / 113
New Mexico	505 265-7859	$115.00	215,000	25	??? / 29
New York[2]	518 464-6483	$285.00	1,750,000	25	250 / 250
New York[3]	518 449-1667	$300.00	1,650,000	25	??? / ???
N. Carolina	919 787-7443	$200.00	1,400,000	25	38 / 95
North Dakota	701 223-6397	$119.00	350,000	25	80 / 90
Ohio	614 486-6677	$150.00	912,000	25	46 / 78
Oklahoma	405 524-4421	$225.00	1,800,000	25	155 / 195
Oregon	503 624-6397	$200.00	600,000	25	59 / 77
Pennsylvania	717 234-4067	$300.00	2,500,000	25	?? / 160
S. Carolina	803 254-1607	$220.00	808,000	25	?? / 79
South Dakota	605 692-4300	$135.00	385,000	25	130 / 141
Tennessee	615 584-5761	$115.00	560,000	25	55 / 70
Texas	512 477-6755	$300.00	1,700,000	25	265 / 300
Utah	801 328-8678	$115.00	400,000	25	42 / 45
Virginia	804 550-2361	$225.00	1,500,000	25	72 / 92
Washington	206 634-3838	$175.00	951,000	25	98 / 100
West Virginia	304 342-1011	$150.00	648,000	25	47 / 62
Wisconsin	608 238-7171	$195.00	1,400,000	25	200 / 221
Wyoming	307 745-8144	$119.00	181,000	25	31 / 39

Notes: 1. New England States include: MA, ME, NH, VT, RI, CT
2. New York Press Association
3. New York News Publishers Association

TRAVEL PREMIUMS / INCENTIVES

Contact the following four companies about their travel incentive packages, as discussed in Chapter Two. They may have other incentive packages as well, such as savings coupon books.

Adler Travel
638 Marsolan Ave.
Solana Beach, CA 92075
(800) 442-3537) OR (619) 793-0629
http://www.freetravel.com/

Fennell Promotions, Inc.
6640 Powers Ferry Road, Suite 175
Atlanta, GA 30339
800-969-4115
Fax: (770) 612-9954
E-Mail: info@fennellpromotions.com
http://www.fennellpromotions.com/

Crown Marketing Group, Inc.
17755 US Highway 19 North
Clearwater, FL 34624
(813) 535-6600
E-mail: info@crownmarketing.com
http://www.crownmarketing.com/index.html

Premium Exchange, Inc.
1698 Lower Roswell Road
Marietta, GA 30068
(770) 973-2784
Fax #: (770) 565-1996
E-mail:premex@randomc.com
http://www.premex.com/

DJC Enterprises
3653 Slopeview Drive
San Jose, CA 95148
(408) 238-5610
Fax #: (408) 238-5610
E-mail: cotriss@inow.com
http://www.djcenterprises.com

PROMOTIONAL ITEMS

If you are interested in some of the more traditional promotional items (most with your company information imprinted on them at your request), check out the following address for a list of over 200 suppliers:

http://www.yahoo.com/Business_and_Economy/Companies/Marketing/Advertising/Promotional_Items

Here is a small sampling of the different items you can get from these companies:

pencils	pens	caps	mugs
t-shirts	fine china	sunglasses	coasters
pitchers	playing cards	calendars	cigarette lighters
banners	signs	license plates	mouse pads
dust covers	plastic shelves	watches	radios
clocks	flags	balloons	banners
matchbooks	golf clubs	towels	decals
buttons	magnets	foreign coins	medals
plaques	certificates	stamps	letter openers
sweats	tote bags	aprons	tins
bbq grills	fudge	posters	cookbooks
key chains	stuffed animals	jackets	cameras
sweats	tools	compasses	umbrellas
banknotes			

VOICE MAIL SERVICES

Before doing anything else, check with your local telephone company. BellSouth charges just over $5.00 for their voice mail service, and I expect other phone companies have similar plans. Failing that, look in your yellow pages under "Answering Services" or "Voice Messaging."

The company I use for fax reception, FaxWeb, also offers voice mail service for an additional $5.00 / month or $10.00 / month if you use a different phone number than that used for your fax. See the fax-reception resources page for contact information.

In addition, here are some other voice mail companies for you to check out:

Concord Communications: 800-775-7790

This company actually transcribes your voice mail messages and send them to you by e-mail or fax. They charge 39 cents per lead for this transcription service. This is a great service, but unfortunately you also have to pay for toll-free voice mail service—another $9.95/month + 25 cents per minute. Leads can start to get fairly expensive when you add it all up, but it might be worth it if you are qualifying your prospects somewhat before they call.

American Voice Mail *(Ask them about tele-seminar services too.)*
http://www.americanvoice-mail.com/
1-800-347-2861

This company sets you up with a local voice mail number just about anywhere in the U.S. Prices start at $9.95 per month with no per-minute charges. They also have toll-free voice mail for $4.95/month + 10.9 cents per minute. I used this company in the past and was happy with the service. This is totally unrelated, but just FYI, they also have prepaid calling cards starting at 17 cents per minute . . . not bad!

Growth Curve *(With Interactive Voice Mail!)*
E-mail: Mail@growthcurve.com
WWW: http://www.growthcurve.com

Growth Curve offers a multitude of voice mail services. Standard voice mail can be purchased for $6.00/month, and it only costs an additional $3.00/month to add question/answer abilities as discussed in Chapter Two. So for $9.00 per month, you could have an interactive order-taking service. This company is definitely worth your consideration.

Voice Text 512-404-2300 *(Call about their Tele-seminar services.)*

TOLL-FREE ORDER TAKING SERVICES

If you don't have a storefront (if you only sell by the mail or online), then toll-free order taking is a necessity. There are reports of sales more than DOUBLING when this option was added to the sales materials. The companies below are used by many direct marketers throughout the U.S. and Canada, and you should receive good service from any of them.

Extend Communications Inc.
E-mail: info@extendcomm.com
WWW: http://www.extendcomm.com
519-759-6820
800-265-9975

This is the company I use—good service and excellent prices. They really cater to the entrepreneur and are very popular in the direct marketing circles.

Mountain West Communications, Inc.
800-642-9378

Though I haven't used them personally, this company has also been highly recommended by several well-known direct marketers.

Star-Byte, Inc.
http://www.starbyte.com/sales.html
(800) 243-1515 (Ask for their *Order Taking and Fulfillment Services* Bulletin)

Star-Byte will stock your products, take incoming 800-line orders, process credit card information (using their merchant account), and send the order out. They charge $3.00 + actual postage costs to take and fulfill the order, and they have a $100 monthly minimum. Credit card orders incur a 2.9% transaction fee. All in all, not a bad deal.

SecrePhone
1-800-727-4599 (ask for Sergio)

This company was recommended to me by one of their customers. They only charge $20/month + $0.20 / minute. The phone is first answered by a computer, a short message is played, and then a live operator comes on the line to take the order. I have no experience with this company, but if you're looking for a low-cost way to get started, you might want to consider them.

FAX RECEIVING SERVICES

If you are going to be receiving orders or other important information by fax, then you don't want to run the risk of the caller getting a busy signal. You want a 24 hour, multi-line fax reception service. My first recommendation is that you check your local yellow pages and call around for prices—look under "Telecommunications" or "Answering Services"—you may find a local company that gives you even more flexibility than the national ones.

If you can't find anything local, here are some other options:

FaxWeb
E-mail: support@faxweb.net
WWW: http://www.faxweb.net/
(770) 451-0024

This is the company I use, and my experience with them was very good. They charge $15 per month for my own unique FAX phone number, and notify me by e-mail whenever I receive a fax. I view and/or download the received faxes using my web browser. For an extra $5/month they provide voice-mail service that I can also access via the web—a really a slick operation. I never had a problem with their service and highly recommend them. Note: If you don't have web access, you won't be able to use this service.

OmniTelesys
E-mail: info@igconcepts.com
(847) 824-5511

This company charges $5.00 per month for their fax receiving service (they call it their "Fax Mailbox" service). On top of the flat fee, they charge on a per-page basis if you have the faxes forwarded to your fax machine. You can also get sofware that allows you to call up their system and download your fax messages with your computer. I imagine this would be considerably less expensive—contact them for pricing details.

Business Link International
E-mail: sales@blifax.com
FOD: 1-800-811-7805 (call from your fax machine!)

This company charges $9.95 per month for receiving up to 25 pages. Received faxes sent to you as an attachment to an e-mail message. They charge 20 cents per page for any pages over 25.

FAX ON DEMAND (FOD) COMPANIES

I was surprised at how difficult it is to find reasonably priced FOD services! One company I called wanted to charge $500 for the setup, plus $100/month minimum. Obviously, they're used to working with the huge companies that spend that much without giving it a second thought. The fax on demand services of the two companies below, however, are quite reasonable—well within the budget of any business.

Fax Power Fax-on-Demand
E-mail: adagent@ibmc.com

This FOD company charges $60 per year (payment in advance) for up to a 10 page document. One catch is that they collect the fax numbers of the people who call and request your document—they most likely rent, sell, or otherwise use these numbers to make more money.

The e-mail address and web site address given above are for a distributor of this company. They advertise their services via network marketing.

Growth Curve *(With Interactive Voice Mail)*
E-mail: Mail@growthcurve.com
WWW: http://www.growthcurve.com

Growth Curve offers fax on demand for $6.00 per page per month—or $4.00 per page per month if you use any of their other services (i.e. voice mail, interactive voice mail, audio brochure). They also offer a "deluxe" fax on demand that captures prospect information before sending the fax. The cost is $10/page/month (or $7/page/month if you use any of their other services).

Incor Enterprises Inc.
E-mail:webmaster@incor.com
WWW: http://www.incor.com/inc_fod.htm

Incor requires a 6 or 12 month payment in advance. 6 months is $40 ($6.67/month), 12 months is $60.00 ($5.00/month). This is for 3 pages on your FOD system. Additional pages are $20 each.

ACCEPTING CREDIT CARDS

Being able to accept credit cards goes hand in hand with using toll-free ordering. People love to use plastic, and will order things with their credit cards that otherwise they might not. Virtually all direct marketing impulse spending is done with a credit card and a toll free order line. You've got to have both to compete . . . possibly just to survive!

Here's a quote from something I read online recently:

> *Unless you have been in business for 2 years with a Dunn and Bradstreet referral, two years of tax returns, "A paper" credit rating and probably several other hoops, you will have very little chance, if any at all, of getting Merchant Account Software for Major Credit Card acceptance for your business or individual use.*

All I can say to that is **BALONEY!** The people responsible for the above statement were trying to make small business owners believe the only way they were going to get a credit card merchant account was through this company—at an outrageous cost of $1,800. Just about anyone with decent credit can get a merchant account. Even if you have bad credit there are ways around it. If for some reason you just can't get your own merchant account, take heart—there are other ways you can cash in on the plastic craze. In fact, there are actually some advantages to some of the alternatives.

Below are some of the companies that will work with you to get your own merchant account, as well as some companies that make it possible to profit from credit card orders without having a merchant account.

Getting your own credit card merchant account

Wells Fargo Bank
http://wellsfargo.com/biz/merchant

I have a friend that got a merchant account through Wells Fargo. They seem to be treating him fairly, and the didn't charge him an arm and a leg for their services.

Merchants Choice Card Services
http://The.Emporium.net/Approved/Default.html

I just had to include this one. Branches Mall has a web page for referring prospects to CardService International (a very well-known company in this industry). On their web page they state: "Everyone qualifies—even if you have been turned down before. Home business, internet business or new business. No exceptions and no application fee." They further go on to state: "Everyone qualifies and will be approved regardless of credit history." In order to get this "guaranteed acceptance" you have to inform CardService Intl. that you were referred by Branches Mall. I have a hard time believing this guarantee, but hey, it's worth a shot.

EMS Global / Sheila Danzig
http://www.charge.com

I really resisted putting this resource in here, because their processing equipment and/or software costs so much. Just for comparison, I think my friend that got his account through Wells Fargo paid about $350 for his software—this company wants $995 for their software. I'm sure Ms. Danzig gets a healthy chunk of that as her referral fee. However, they are one of the first companies to do this, and they do seem to have success in securing merchant accounts for those who don't mind paying the exhorbitant price.

Teleflora CreditLine
E-mail: HYTUARTE@ATTMAIL.COM
WWW: http://www.creditline.com/index.htm
(800) 321-2654 ext 4534

This company has been highly recommended by a number of people . They supply a LOT of people with merchant accounts. They don't publish their rates, but I've been told they are very reasonable. Contact them for a quote, you may be pleasantly surprised.

COSTCO (yes, Costco)

I am quoting this information directly from Bill Myers' online discussion group:

> *If you have a Costco store nearby consider their offer for an Executive membership account. It comes as a basket of small business services including group medical, auto and home insurance and rebates on real estate transactions. Merchant credit card services are part of this. It's an upgrade of membership that costs $100/yr rather than the regular $30/yr. You can then use any of these additional business services.*
>
> *OK here's the deal on credit card processing: No monthly fees, and a 2.14% rate plus $0.15 each on Internet transactions. (1.59% rate if you physically have and can swipe the card). Rent or buy the software (I don't have prices on this). Available to new or existing businesses. Offers Visa and Mastercard.*

See how much useful information can be found at these discussion groups?

Taking plastic even WITHOUT a merchant account

Mountain West Communications, Inc.
(800) 642-9378

Give these people a call. If you contract with them to handle your inbound order taking and order fulfillment work, they may also process credit card transactions for you—depending on your product. They've been burned by some "paper product" companies before.

Star-Byte, Inc.
http://www.starbyte.com/sales.html
(800) 243-1515 (Ask for their *Order Taking and Fulfillment Services* Bulletin)

Star-Byte will stock your products, take incoming 800-line orders, process credit card information (using their merchant account), and send the order out. They charge $3.00 + actual postage costs to take and fulfill the order, and they have a $100 monthly minimum. Credit card orders incur a 2.9% transaction fee. All in all, not a bad deal.

All of the next few companies are web-based—you need to have access to the web to use their services. All but Octagon Technology Group require that your customer has web access as well. With the exception of Octagon (I'll explain their unique position later), these companies act as resellers for your product. They agree to purchase your product for some value less than the retail cost, and to then sell it to the customer at retail.

Here's generally how it works. The customer visits your web site and determines that they want to make a purchase using their credit card. They are sent to a "secure order form" on the reseller's site, and they place the order. They have just become the customer for the reseller. The reseller sends the customer a receipt and forwards the order to you for you to ship (commonly referred to as a "*drop-ship*" order). Technically, the delivered package should bear the name of the reseller.

There is a reason these companies must become resellers of your product. If one company just processes credit card transactions for another company, it is considered "factoring" which is forbidden by the credit card companies; this practice could cost a company its merchant account. However, it is perfectly legitimate for a company to buy merchandise from you and resell it to someone else.

Internet Billing Company
http://www.ibill.com/index.html

Though their transaction fee is higher than some of the others, this is one of the few companies with no setup or monthly/yearly service charges. They charge 15% of the order as their commission, and hold back an additional 10% for six months in order to cover any chargebacks that might occur.

Multicards
http://www.multicards.com

This company charges $150/year up to $700/year depending on which commission percentage you choose—the percentage ranges from 6% to 10%. Checks are sent two weeks after the Monday following an order.

Octagon Technology Group, Inc.
http://www.otginc.com/

Rather than acting as a reseller, Octagon becomes your advocate with the credit card companies and banks. They set up a merchant account in your company's name, and act as a guarantor of that account which is similar to co-signing a loan.

All orders are placed through their web server. One big advantage with Octagon: if you have offline customers and orders, you can manually enter those orders on a special page designed just for your use. The other companies can't allow this, as it would violate the reseller relationship.

Octagon charges $650 to set up your account (includes last month fee), $50 Monthly miniumum, $0.50 per transaction + 5-6% of retail amount depending on volume. They also have 1-800 inbound order taking services to augment the web-based ordering system, at additional cost.

MoneyIn
http://www.moneyin.com

This company charges $150 for setup, and 10% commission on all orders.

SecureCC
http://www.securecc.com/price.html

SecureCC has no setup fee, but they do have a $100/month minimum on a 10% commission rate.

Secure800
http://www.secure800.com/overview.html

This company's service is unique. When your customer decides to place an order, they fill out an online form and hit the "send" button. They are then given a 10 digit code and an 800 number to call. They call the 800 number, enter the code when prompted, and then enter their credit card information. This completes the transaction. Secure800 has a $99.00 setup fee, and a per-order charge of 5.5% + $1.00 ($3.50 minimum total).

ACCEPTING CHECK BY PHONE/FAX

I have accepted checks by phone, fax, e-mail, and web site. It can be handy when you need it, let me tell you. There are two ways of converting check information to a depositable check. The first way is to have a service bureau process the information and cut you a check, less their fee. One such company is:

Mid American Financial Group
http://www.choicemall.com/phonechecks/
FAX: 1-608-883-9957
They charge $25 to set you up, and then $1.25 per check.

The second way is to use software specifically designed for converting the required information into checks you can deposit. There are many different "Fax-Check" software programs out there, ranging from $14.95 to $299 or more. I listed two sources below for the "Checker" software:

Real Marketing
E-mail: Ram1933137@aol.com
http://www.real-marketing.com/checker.html

Dave (who runs this site) was running a special on this software through 1/1/98, and he agreed to extend that offer indefinitely to the readers of this guide. The special price is $25.00, and you can download a demo version of the software right from his site.

David Munn
http://www.freeyellow.com/members/check/

This is the lowest price I've found (so far) for Fax/Phone Check software—just $14.95.

CHARGING ORDERS TO THE PHONE BILL

Do you have a product that can be sold for $2.00 to $35.00? If so, there are a couple of companies you can use to charge these orders to your customer's phone bill. Typically, the customer will call the 1-900 number, will receive a code, and with that code will be able to access a password-protected area of a web site, either to view the content there, or to download a file.

What if your product is more tangible? You'll have to check with the companies listed below, but you may be able to get around this by adding an information product or software product as a BONUS to your main product. Or, you could swap. Make the information/software your main product, and send the "hard" product as a bonus. The customer would be able to download the electronic product and use it while waiting for your "tangible" product to be delivered by conventional methods.

Internet Billing Company
http://www.ibill.com/index.html

If this name look familiar, it's because you saw it in the previous section. This company also has a "Web900" program whereby they allow customer purchases via a 1-900 number. They have no setup fee, and charge 20% commission for their service. Their product price points are $2, $4.95, $5.95, $7.95, $9.95, $10, $12, $15, $19.95, $25, $30 or $35. Your product must sell at one of those price points.

Register Online

Register Online was originally conceived as a way for shareware software authors to increase registration of their software by making it easy for the customer. They now allow straight purchase of software as well. Price points are: $4.95, $5.95, $7.95, $10.00, $12.00, $15.00, $19.95, $25.00, $30.00, $35.00.

FREE E-MAIL SERVICES

Every web site comes with an e-mail address, but there may be cases where you need to get a different e-mail address—a "backup" e-mail account, or a private account. Whatever the reason, you should have no difficulty obtaining an extra (or two or three) e-mail address. Several possible options are listed below, and all except Juno require WWW access:

Juno
http://www.juno.com
(800) 654-5866

note

Juno is the only service that allows you to send and receive e-mail without having any internet service. It is totally free—the costs of maintaing the Juno service are offset by advertising that you receive along with your e-mail messages.

FreeYellow
http://www.freeyellow.com

Friendly E-mail
http://www.thekeyboard.com

GeoCities
http://www.geocities.com

GoPlay
http://www.goplay.com

Hotmail
http://www.hotmail.com

MailCity
http://www.mailcity.com

NetAddress
http://www.netaddress.usa.net

RocketMail
http://www.rocketmail.com

Yahoo! Mail
http://www.yahoo.com

DIRECT "OPT-IN" E-MAIL ADVERTISING SERVICES

Bullet Mail
http://www.bulletmail.com

This company has 75 different categories, and charges 5 to 6 cents for each e-mail address they e-mail on your behalf. Their lists are pretty small, in the 2,000-6,000 range, and you have to mail to an entire list at once (no testing of 1,000 names). Because of the small cost, this may be a good company to use for a test. If it is profitable, then you can try one of the bigger companies with their $300.00 minimum.

BusinessLink's Targeted E-mail
http://www.targetede-mail.com

Over 600,000 e-mail addresses in over 4,000 categories. Business Link charges 10 to 35 cents for each e-mail they send in your behalf, and they have a minimum order of $300.00.

Multimedia Marketing Group
http://www.mmgco.com/adniche.html

This company actually brokers advertising on E-mail lists. They will analyze your product/service, determine the best e-mail lists to advertise in, write the advertising copy, place the ads, and provide an autoresponder service for the resulting inquiries. Contact them directly to inquire about costs.

Postmaster Direct
http://www.postmasterdirect.com

Over 3 million e-mail addresses in over 7,000 categories. Postmaster Direct also has a $300.00 minimum. I couldn't find a stated range of costs on their web site anywhere, but the range I've personally seen is 7 to 20 cents each. Most categories are 15 cents each.

LIST SERVER (E-MAIL LIST) SERVICES

Many web hosting companies include a list server as part of their standard web hosting package. Others charge a nominal ($5 to $25) monthly fee. If you are shopping for a web site host, be sure to keep availability and cost of this service in mind when making comparisons.

If your web hosting provider doesn't include this kind of service, or if it's very expensive, here are some companies that will host your list at reasonable prices:

Expert Internet Service
E-mail: drummond@xpert.net
WWW:http://www.xpert.net

This company charges $30/month for their list server service, but they don't state if that is for unlimited usage or not. Ask before signing up!

mail-list.com
E-mail: mdm@mail-list.com
WWW: http://www.mail-list.com

$9.95/month for a small list, $99.95/month for a large list (a mailing to 4000 people per week was considered small, I don't know where the line is drawn between small and large.)

Sun Coast Web
E-mail: information@clearwaterfl.com
WWW: http://clearwaterfl.com/domo.htm

This company charges on a "per e-mail" basis. For every e-mail you send, they charge $0.0015. This means you can send 1,000 e-mail messages for $1.50. What this means to me is that if I sent out an announcement to all my e-mail list subscibers (4,000 of them) once per week, it would cost me 4,000 X 4 weeks X $0.0015 = $24.00 for a month of service. There is a $10 minimum monthly charge.

Worldprofit
E-mail:drjlant@worldprofit.com

Worldprofit requires that you pay for 12 months at a time, at a rate of $400/year ($33.33/month) for unlimited usage.

AUTORESPONDER SERVICES

As with many of the other internet services, check first with your web host provider. Many accounts come with 1, 2, 10 or even unlimited autoresponders. If you don't have enough autoresponders (or the right kind) as part of your standard hosting service, these companies should be able to help you:

BusinessLink
http://www.businesslink.net/autoresponders.html

$39/year for one, or $125/year for 5 autoresponders. This company also has an autoresponder service allowing you to include binary attachments to your outgoing files! Cost for this service is $149/year (1 MEG files or smaller).

E-mail Xpress
http://www.141.com

If cost is your only concern, I doubt you'll find anyone cheaper than E-mail Xpress—$5.00 setup charge and only $2.00/month (12 month minimum, paid in advance).

InfoBack
http://www.infoback.net/

This company's prices start at $9.95/month for a single autoresponder. If you get 10 autoresponders and take advantage of some other savings plans, you can get the price below $6.00/month for each one.

MailBack
http://www2.databack.com/mailback

This company has some great ideas. They offer a standard autoresponder for $6/month. They also offer a "2-step" autoresponder—it sends a message immediately, and then automatically follows up 1 week later with a different message. They even have a "multi-step" autoresponder that will follow up at regular intervals (you specify how many times and how much time in-between)—a direct marketers dream machine! They have other creative and beneficial services too. Do yourself a favor and check them out.

MARKETING E-MAIL LISTS and E-ZINES

Here are a few of the MANY e-mail lists and e-zines related to marketing. Subscriptions are all free. Just go to the listed web site address and sign-up. Several of these allow paid advertising and advertising in this medium can be some of the most cost effective marketing available. So, check into it.

BizBotWeekly
http://www.bizbotweekly.com/subscribe.html

BizWeb Gazette
http://www.bizweb2000.com/sample.htm

Entrepreneurs Weekly
http://www.eweekly.com

Gator Byte
http://www.gatorsbyte.com/default.htm

OakNet News
http://www.oaknetpub.com

Web Marketing Today
http://www.wilsonweb.com/wmt

Worldgram Newsletter
http://www.worldprofit.com/fmcatalg.htm

To find other interesting and useful E-mail Lists and E-Zines, check out these web sites:

Vivian Neou's List of Lists
http://catalog.com/vivian/interest-group-search.html

Publicly Accessible Mailing Lists
http://www.neosoft.com/internet/paml

Liszt, The Mailing List Directory
http://www.liszt.com

eZines Ultimate Magazine Database
http://www.dominis.com/Zines/

MARKETING-RELATED NEWSGROUPS

I have listed various marketing and small business related newsgroups below. It used to be that you could come to these newsgroups for some very good discussions about various business issues. Now the advertising static overwhelms everything else—if there is even anyone taking the time to post worthwhile messages. These groups may be of use to you, however, in discovering new marketing tools and services, since they are filled with advertisements about anything and everything business related.

If you want to use newsgroups to generate leads, I suggest you find a newsgroup about your specific niche and participate in the discussions there. Include your tasteful and appropriate SIG file at the end of every message you post, of course. You can also post useful articles to these groups, and include your contact information (as long as it isn't a blatant violation of the newsgroup's "no advertising" policy).

Technically, most of the below newgroups don't allow advertising either, but they appear to have deteriorated into a state of advertising chaos:

alt.biz.misc
alt.business
alt.business.home
alt.business.home.pc
alt.business.misc
alt.business.multi-level
alt.commerce.misc-ads
alt.internet.commerce
alt.www.marketing
alt.www.marketing.adverts
biz.general
biz.marketplace
biz.misc
biz.mlm
biz.next.newprod
market.internet.free
misc.business
misc.business.marketing
misc.entrepreneurs
tnn.marketing.internet

E-Z TIP

If you have a specific interest and want to find out if there are any related newsgroups, the best place to try is:

DejaNews: http://www.dejanews.com

MARKETING DISCUSSION GROUPS

These discussion groups contain a wealth of information—some of the very best direct marketers visit these sites and unselfishly share their trade secrets. These people have made millions of dollars, so it pays to listen to what they have to say. Don't be intimidated. Go ahead and ask your questions, share your observations—this is a very friendly bunch and they know that everyone has something to teach the rest of us. Visit them all.

Bill Myers's Independent Publishers Discussion Group
http://www.bmyers.com/ipub/index.html

The above is the top discussion group on my list. They talk about anything having to do with entrepreneurship and independence, not just publisher's issues. Some of the information in this guide was brought to light on this discussion board. Visit it often.

Anthony Blake's Entrepreneurial Success Forum
http://www.ablake.com/cgi-bin/index.cgi

Thomas Bererton's Webprofits Discussion Group
http://www.position-it.com/wp

Wilson Internet Services' Web Marketing Forum
http://www.wilsoninet.com/hn/forum

HelpTalk Online Web Promotion Support
http://www.helptalk.com/promote/index.html

Inc. Online's Marketing Forum
http://www.inc.com/bbs/list/13

YOUR OWN WEB SITE—LOW COST OR FREE!

Just like all technology, the cost of your own website has plummeted in the past few years. I was recently pricing web hosting services and one of the "front runners" in my search offers the following package:

- 100 Megabytes Disk Storage
- my own domain name ("www.myname.com" instead of "www.theirname.com/~myname/")
- up to 4 POP e-mail addresses
- unlimited Traffic (they don't charge extra if I get too many visitors to my site)
- unlimited "virtual" e-mail addresses
- unlimited AUTORESPONDERS
- listServe Service
- installed scripts for:
    - guestbook
    - discussion group
    - form handler
    - shopping cart
- full CGI script support for custom scripts
- secured server

And the cost? Just $24.95 per month. Theirs wasn't even the lowest price package. Incredible!

There's no way I can list even a good sample of the many available web hosting companies in this guide, but I can point you to a couple of online sources:

The Ultimate Web Host List
http://www.webhostlist.com

I especially like the "Top 25" list this site updates on a monthly basis. You're probably pretty safe if you go with one of these companies.

Host Search
http://www.hostsearch.com

This site allows you to enter the parameters you are most concerned with (price, capabilities, etc.) and then gives you a list of the web hosting companies that best fit your needs.

Both of the above web sites have resources to help you determine what is important when looking for your own web hosting service. Read up on it, and then let the search begin.

In addition to the sites you pay for, there are several places where you can get your own FREE website. These web sites aren't going to allow you near the flexibility and capability as one you pay for, but they can be useful in your marketing efforts.

One excellent way to make use of these free sites is using them to "funnel" web traffic to your main site. Because they are at different locations on the internet, you can list them all in the search engines. When people go to the free site, you give them some good information, whet their appetite for more, and direct them to visit your main site. By the way, many of the below companies provide you with an e-mail address to go with your free web site.

Angelfire Communications
http://www.angelfire.com

Angelfire only gives you 200 kilobytes of disk space for your website. That's enough for a very simple site which you can use to send people to your main site, but that's about it. They do provide ample help for creating your web page there.

Focus Asia
http://www.focus-asia.com

Free Asia provides you with 2 megabytes of disk space for your web site.

Free Yellow
http://www.freeyellow.com/shoestring

Free Yellow only allows you 5 pages for your web site, but they have a lot of other features too, like an autoresponder, the ability to have your visitors fill out and send you a form, a discussion group (they call it a message board) and more. Pretty nifty.

GeoCities
http://www.geocities.com/join/freehp.html

Geocities is one of the largest and most recognized of the free web site providers. You get 3 megabytes of disk storage and lots of help. If you want to upgrade later, you can—starting at $4.95 for 15 megabytes of storage.

Max Pages
http://maxpages.com/

This site requires you to make your pages using their page building utilities (online). Max Pages doesn't create true HTML files, but keeps everything in a database and renders each site and page as it is requested. Though you can't upload your own graphics and files yet, they have plans to add that capability. Max Pages allows you up to 50 pages in your web site.

OneStop Network
http://home.onestop.net/

You get 2 Megs for your homepage, FTP uploads, and a homepage hit counter. When I last checked, they had over 10,000 people with free web sites there.

TaoTree Free Web Services
http://www.tou.com/host

TaoTree offers 3 Megs of disk space for your web site, and they also offer free autoresponders, guestbooks, counters, and CGI forms support. Unfortunately, when I last checked they had stopped accepting new accounts. They're looking for more resources before they add anyone else. Check their site from time to time until they start accepting new members again.

Tripod
http://www.tripod.com/planet/membership/signup

Tripod has been around for a long time, and theirs is one of the more "polished" services. They have a utility that allows anyone to create their web page even without knowing HTML. If you DO know HTML and want a fine-tuned site, you can do that too. Tripod allows you 2 megabytes of disk space.

WebSpawner
http://www.webspawner.com/

Rather than a web site, WebSpawner allows you one web page—less than anyone else, but still enough to get you some traffic. Besides, how can anyone complain—it's free!

Xoom
http://www.xoom.com

Xoom offers you a whopping 5 megabytes of disk storage for you web site. You can make a LOT of web pages with that (100 easily).

WWW-RELATED SOFTWARE and CGI SCRIPTS

Netscape
http://www.netscape.com

Internet Explorer
http://www.microsoft.com

These are the two most popular web browsers (what you use to view web sites) and there is no reason to get anything else, since these are free. Chances are that at least one of these is on your computer already. These programs can also be used to send and receive your e-mail.

Web Promotion Spider
http://www.servers-unlimited.com/spider/

This program allows you to register your web site with several hundred (last I checked it was 407) different search engines, indices, directories, and free ad sites. You can download a working copy of it (only registers with 5 sites). If you like it, you can purchase a password that will enable you to remove this limitation.

WebExpress
http://www.mvd.com/

note

If you have absolutely ZERO experience with HTML coding (web site creation) and you want to make a basic website fast, this is a great little program to have. You won't have to learn any HTML tag codes, if you can use a word processor, you can use this program to build your first web page. The trial version is free to download.

HomeSite
http://www.allaire.com/

This program has a little more power than WebExpress, and the tradeoff is that it is a bit more complex. If you have a more time to learn how to use it, this might be the software for you. This program can also be downloaded on a free trial basis, so if you aren't sure which one is best for you, get them both and try them out. Keep the one you like most.

Microsoft FrontPage
http://www.microsoft.com

Adobe PageMill
http://www.adobe.com

These are two of the "big guys" in web site design. They allow you to "drag and drop" words and pictures to make your web pages. Frontpage also has some advanced site management capabilities. These programs are powerful, but have a learning curve. If you have the time and will to learn them, they might be better tools than the simpler ones shown above.

CGI Scripts

Recall from Chapter Two that "Custom Forms" are controlled with scripts—CGI scripts (written in the PERL programming language, usually) to be exact. The great thing about scripts is that most if not all the scripts you need are free. The FIRST thing you should do is check with your ISP (internet service provider). MANY (if not most) ISPs install standard scripts for you, including a guestbook script and a mailform script.

If you don't have an ISP, this might be something for you to consider when you are evaluating your many choices for one. If you already have an ISP and they don't have or install any scripts for you, then here are the scripts you'll want along with a short description of what they do. All of these scripts can be found at one or more (probably all three) of these web sites:

CGI Resources
http://www.cgi-resources.com/Programs_and_Scripts/Perl

FreeCode
http://www.freecode.com

Matt's Script Archive
http://www.worldwidemart.com/scripts

These scripts are just the tip of the iceberg. Browse through the above sites and you'll be amazed at the variety of scripts available to you to use free of charge. Another very useful link is:

http://www.scriptsearch.com

Guestbook Script

A *guestbook* allows you to set up your own comments page. Visitors to your site can add comments to your guestbook as well as reading the comments of others. This is a good way to get feedback about your website.

WWWboard (discussion group) Script

This is the script I talked about in Chapter Two (and Three too). Remember, a discussion group is like a web-based bulletin board. People come to your discussion group page, post messages (new ones or replies to existing messages), and read what others have to say. I suppose you could consider it a guestbook with expanded features. Namely the ability to reply to someone else's comments. It allows a threaded discussion, rather than just a bunch of individual, unrelated comments.

Mailform Script

When you create "forms" to collect prospect or customer information—such as the registration form I showed you in Chapter Two—you need some way of getting that data sent from the web page (where the form resides) to your e-mail address. That's what the MAILFORM script does. When people click on the "Send" or "Submit" button (you can call it whatever you want) the form data is intercepted by this script, formatted, and sent to you as an e-mail message.

INTERNET-SEARCHING SITES

If you want to find something on the Internet, there are several search engines and directories available to help you. As with all other things, different search tools should be used for different needs. If you're just going to browse different categories of interest, use Yahoo! If you are looking for a particular article in the newsgroups, the only tool I would recommend is DejaNews.

Dogpile, Inference Find!, and Northern Light (possibly others, too) are very useful if you want to search multiple engines and directories simultaneously. Infoseek has given me excellent references when I just wanted to do a search on a key word. Yahoo! does pretty good here too.

If you want to search for keywords embedded as "meta tags" in documents, try AltaVista, Hotbot, Infoseek and MetaCrawler.

Alta Vista	http://www.altavista.digital.com
DejaNews	http://www.dejanews.com
Dogpile	http://www.dogpile.com
Excite	http://www.excite.com
HotBot	http://www.hotbot.com
Inference Find!	http://www.inference.com/ifind
Infoseek	http://www.infoseek.com
LookSmart	http://www.looksmart.com
Lycos	http://www.lycos.com
Magellan	http://www.mckinley.com
MetaCrawler	http://www.metacrawler.com
Nothern Light	http://www.northernlight.com
Snap!	http://home.snap.com
Starting Point	http://www.stpt.com
WebCrawler	http://webcrawler.com
Yahoo!	http://www.yahoo.com

This last link isn't a search engine or directory, but it is a handy site to visit if you want to keep up on what the search engines are doing. You can also put your name on an "update me by e-mail" list:

Search Engine Watch
http://searchenginewatch.com

WEB SITES YOU SHOULD VISIT

General Small Business, Home Business, or Marketing-related web sites

These web sites have good information for the small business owner, especially related to marketing, internet marketing, and web promotion. Almost all of these sites have free reports that contain a wealth of useful information for online AND offline business activities. Each one also has numerous links to other relevant web sites—so much information, so little time to absorb it all!

Advanced Web Marketing	http://www.fenet.co.uk/awm
BizHub	http://www.bizhub.com
Blake Marketing Group	http://www.ablake.com
Copywriting Profit Center	http://www.mrfire.com/Knowledge/Copywriting/index.html
Cyberwave Media	http://www.cyberwave.com
Forerunner Business Group	http://www.forerunnergroup.com
Free marketing reports	http://www.infoback.net/freebizopps/freerep.htm
Gebbie Press	http://www.gebbieinc.com
HelpTalk	http://www.helptalk.com/index.html
IceMall How-To Reports	http://www.icemall.com/reports/index.html
Inc. Online	http://www.inc.com
Marketing Resource Info Center	http://www.marketingresource.com
NFIB Online	http://www.nfibonline.com
Position-It	http://www.position-it.com
Small Business Advisor	http://www.isquare.com/fhome13.htm
Small Biz	http://www.techweb.com/smallbiz
SmallOffice.com	http://www.smalloffice.com
Smart Business Supersite	http://www.smartbiz.com
Standard Rate and Data Service	http://www.srds.com
Web Marketing Forum	http://www.wilsoninet.com/hn/forum
Web Success Letter	http://www.writething.com
Window of Opportunity	http://www.uni-sol.com/window
Winning with Small Business	http://www.success.org/wwsbc

Internet Promotion Web Sites

Earlier in this chapter I showed you some software that allows you to create web pages without knowing HTML. However, it's always a good thing to know if you want to "fine tune" your web pages. If you go to any search engine (I use Yahoo for this one myself) and enter the keywords "HTML Tutorial" or "Learn HTML" you have all the help you need. But, just to get you started, here's the link to the *Beginners Guide to HTML:*

http://www.ncsa.uiuc.edu/general/internet/www/HTMLPrimer.html

I showed you some of the headline testing I did using LinkExchange. They are one of the best-known and most used link exchanges, and their web site address is:

http://www.linkexchange.com

For many other banner exchanges, go to the following Yahoo! web page:

http://www.yahoo.com/Computers_and_Internet/Internet World_Wide_Web/Announcement_Services/Banner_Exchanges

MediaBuilder Banner Creator
http://www.mediabuilder.com/abm.html

Remember, for best performance in the "big" search engines, you should submit your web site manually. But if you want to submit your site to a lot of directories and search engines in a short period of time, here are some places that will help. Prices vary from free to $625 depending on the service you request and the company supplying it.

Register-It	http://www.register-it.com
Site See	http://www.site-see.com
Submit 200	http://www.bizoffice.com/submit/index.html
Submit-It	http://www.submit-it.com
Virtual Promote	http://www.virtualpromote.com

Before you submit your site, however, you should visit the following sites for some advice:

Meta Checker
http://www.scrubtheweb.com/abs/meta-check.html

This site checks your META tags to make sure you are using them in such a way that the search engines can make the best use of them. Much easier than counting every character yourself.

Position-It
http://www.position-it.com/

This site is full of hints, tips, and tools for making sure your site is ready to be listed with the search engines and to see if your site entry "takes" when you submit it.

Another site you can visit to "check-up" on your own site is:

Web Site Garage
http://www.websitegarage.com

This site gives your home page a score based on how quickly it loaded, how many references to it can be found on the web, spelling, broken links and more. It's a nice utility.

Once you have your site ready to show off, you can send a full press release (via e-mail) to 1200 media outlets for just $225 or just send a less detailed site announcement for $55 by using the Internet News Bureau:

Internet News Bureau
http://www.newsbureau.com

FREE ADVERTISING ON THE INTERNET

There are hundreds or thousands of places where you can place free classified advertisements on the internet. Some marketers say these advertisements aren't worth your time, while others say that their free advertisements generate 50% of the sales volume of their paid advertisements! There are obviously a lot of variables to be considered, but do some testing and see if they work for you.

By the way, a "classifieds" section on your website might be a great way to bring in traffic and there are free scripts available just for that purpose.

Rather than list the individual classified ad sites, I listed several web sites that contain lists of their own. Just point your web browser to these sites and from there you can go to any of several hundred places to submit your own free ad. Once you place an advertisement, be sure to bookmark the site. Keep all your "I placed a classified ad here" bookmarks together in their own bookmark folder—otherwise you'll soon lose track of them.

http://ecki.com/links/

At last count, this site had 2,100 links to free classifieds.

http://www.uran.net/imall/mother.html

This site calls itself "The Mother Of All Classified Links!" and claims to have over 1,000 classified ad sites, search engines and directories. They have both fee-based and free classified sections.

http://www.infoback.net/freebizopps/500free.htm

Over 500 links to free-classified sites can be found here, along with over 200 fee-based sites.

Getting free publicity

5

Chapter 5

Getting free publicity

What you'll find in this chapter:

- Pre- and post-publication requests
- Per-inquiry advertising
- "Till-forbid" advertising rates
- The advantages of co-op advertising
- Testing your promotional package locally

This bonus report is an excerpt from Jeff Gardner's publication, "FREE Advertising Can Make You A Millionaire." I asked Jeff for some material and he sent me the electronic version of his whole book and said, "Please feel free to use any or all of it (or none of it). Use it as you please." How generous! The majority of that publication is reproduced here, but Jeff has some additional information (resources, example forms, etc.) that you may be interested in obtaining. So if you would like to get the whole book, please contact him. His e-mail contact information is: **jgardner@carlsbadnm.com**

It does not matter what business you are in, or whether you are trying to sell products or services, your success depends largely on how well you advertise and publicize what you have to offer.

Advertising and promotional costs can be extremely high, yet no business, large or small, can hope to grow or make profits without some form of advertising.

You could have the best product or service in the world, but if people do not know it is available, they will not send you their money. Needless to say, if you cannot exchange your product for cash, you will not survive.

Not every business can easily afford the luxury of having an adequate advertising budget. You must first achieve some level of success that allows a portion of the profits to work for you in various advertising media.

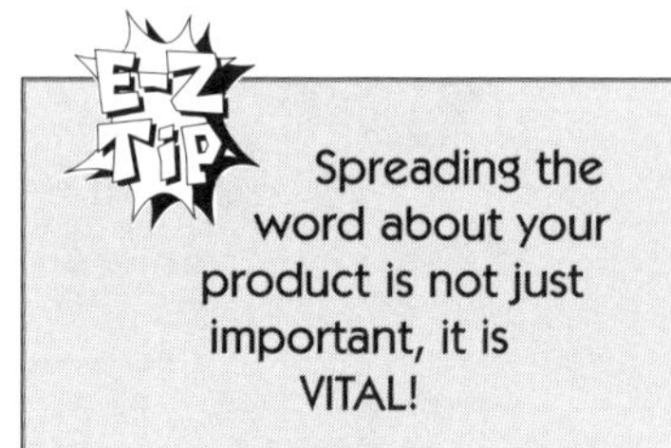

In a sense, it is a Catch-22 situation, in that many entrepreneurs know they cannot make money without advertising, but do not have the money to advertise. Giant corporations spend millions of dollars annually on advertising without blinking an eye. But, their advertising efforts earn them millions in profits. They can afford it. So could a small business if it had the money just to get started. But many do not.

For many businesses in their infancy, just getting set up with office supplies, equipment, and an inventory may not allow any additional funds for a major advertising campaign. For some, it would represent a hardship; for others, an impossibility. Some may say, and rightly so, that "advertising doesn't cost you money, it makes you money." That is true. But, you must have some money at the beginning.

> note
>
> There are enormous opportunities to obtain free advertising and publicity, and give yourself the type of exposure that will make your business grow and prosper.

So what is the answer to this dilemma? The real answer lies in the discovery of how other businesses, no larger than yours, obtained advertising, even though funds did not allow it, and turned their businesses into lucrative and successful ventures. This report provides you with the answers.

Many marketers made a fortune while spending a minimal amount, or nothing, on advertising. The Cabbage Patch Doll is a perfect example of how an item can be sold by the tens and hundreds of thousands, by receiving free publicity. You read about them in the newspapers and magazines, saw them on TV talk shows, saw shoppers lined up waiting for department stores to open their doors on prime time TV news broadcasts. Every child, and the child in adults, just had to have one. And, as live camera pictures showed, they would argue, stampede, drive a hundred miles, and in some cases, even fight to buy one.

note

The first rule of the mail-order business is to "Get as much free advertising and publicity as you can."

All of the paid advertising in the world probably could not have created that buying frenzy. But, free advertising and publicity did!

Publicity is, of course, traditionally free. But, that is no guarantee that your publicity package will ever be put on the air, or placed in print. This report shows you the right approach so that you can enjoy the free publicity your business needs for growth and profits.

How to write an effective news release

A press, or news release, is an effective way to obtain free publicity. There is a distinct difference between an ad and a news release. The primary purpose of an ad is to solicit inquiries or sales. You are promoting a product or service to make a sale. When you write a news release, your ultimate goal is the same, but the approach is quite different.

DEFINITION

A *news release* is just that, news. In a news release you are trying to promote what you have to sell by telling the facts about a product. It should look like news, feel like news, and be news. People read print because the information that is presented is news.

Your news release must somehow be perceived as being useful and benefiting to the readers. That means presenting all of the factual benefits and advantages that your product has to offer.

> **note** Your news release must be interesting and have news value.

Before you can write a news release with the skill of a seasoned newspaper reporter, you have to learn the differences in approach and style that differentiate ads from news releases.

Editors are heroes in print

Editors want to be heroes in the eyes of their readers. They are the people in white hats that protect their readership from anything in print that is not interesting, entertaining, or informational. Whatever goes into print must delight the readers in some way.

To make your news item interesting, you must know all of the benefits and advantages that your product has to offer a reader, and then tie that in with a news interest. You can achieve that by listing every possible benefit your product has, and look at it from a reader's perspective. You must "see" the product and its benefits, as a reader would see it. It does not matter how great you think it is, or what it can do for you. The only thing that is important is what it can do for the reader.

note

Your job is to capture a reader's attention, and create enough interest to have him/her read your complete story. When writing a news release story, your primary focus is to introduce the reader to your product. Your ultimate goal, however, is to prompt an inquiry, and turn a prospect into a customer.

Whether you are writing an ad or a news release, your copy always should address the positive things about your product. Never introduce a negative word, remark, or statement of any kind. If you do, you only use valuable space to overcome the negative remark. For example, if you wrote a book on beauty secrets, and the publication you are promoting in your news release concerns how to look younger with new skin care techniques, it is be better to say *you can look 20 years younger,* than *you no longer have to look old.*

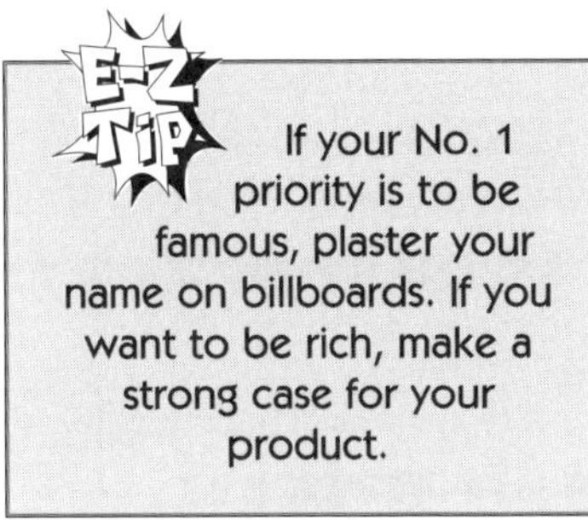

As you develop your news-release copy, always read it from a potential customer's perspective. You not only want your story read, you also want it remembered so vividly that you receive inquiries as a result. Just telling people who you are will not pay the rent. You want action from your publicity, you want to stir up the soup and get things hot and moving.

Everything you write about your company and product should be factual. Never over-exaggerate your claims. People have a built-in sense for gauging what is believable, and what is not. Also, do not make any claims of perfection. You get one shot at establishing your credibility. If you do not come across as honest, sincere, professional, and credible in your story, it probably will not matter. You will never make it past the editor anyway, and the readers, at least in that publication, will never know you exist.

> note
>
> People will not buy perfection, even if you really have somehow achieved it.

Remember, an editor knows why you are submitting your news release. You want free advertising. Editors are not interested in giving anyone a free ad. What they are interested in is filling spaces in newspapers with information that is compatible with their readers' interests. It is vitally important that you know how editors think. Read the article that appeared in a newspaper in August 1991 entitled *The Great Give-away.* The point of this

article is to instill the seriousness with which you must write your news release. Of course, not all editors express their dissatisfaction of free publicity to this extreme. But, it is clear that a news release must be newsworthy, and you must not try to openly sell your product. Most editors will not print it because their business is selling advertising and not buying space for someone else who will make a profit.

Determine where your market is

News releases are not limited to newspapers. There are hundreds of magazines that also have special sections describing what is new on the market.

Before you decide which magazines to send your news release to, you have to analyze your market. *Analyzing your market* means determining who the most likely prospects are for your product, and then deciding which publications are best suited in reaching them.

Once you know who your targeted audience is, and the vehicle you will use to reach them, then you have a good idea of how to formulate your news release. Most magazines also target specific readers. There are boating magazines for boaters, tennis magazines for tennis players, knitting magazines, financial, music, needlecraft, children's, men's, women's, ethnic, opportunity and sales, computer, art, and direct-marketing magazines. There are periodicals and tabloids, and literally hundreds of publications that all appeal to a specific audience.

The point is, if you are selling a book on boating, you do not send your news release to a knitting magazine. And, if you sold men's suspenders, you would not send your release to a woman's magazine. You have to analyze who your market is, and then target that audience.

Once you determine where your market is, and know that your product appeals to a certain publication's readers, it is a good idea to buy a copy of those publications you will send your news release. It is the fastest way to learn if they highlight publicity releases. If they do, you also will see the style and format preferred when they go to print, and the type of items they selected to share with their readers.

To elaborate further on your publication selection, for example, you are selling a new and revolutionary garden tool. Where would you begin? As an example, the *Directory of Leading Magazines and Newspapers* provides you with the names, addresses, and circulation figures. You send your news release, in this instance, to magazines such as *Better Homes and Gardens, Flower and Garden, House and Garden, Country Journal, Horticulture,* etc.

> note
>
> Magazines that you personally like will not bring results. You must select publications that have readers you can tie in with your product.

note

Your magazine copy not only tells you what an editor is looking for in terms of product releases, but also who to write to. Getting your news release to the right person is also important. The editor's name should appear within the first few pages of most publications, or in the section where the news releases appear. The person responsible for that section will usually be soliciting more submissions. That is the person you must address your letter to. Learn all you can about the editor's likes and dislikes by studying what appears in the magazines you will approach. If you know what the editor wants in advance, your chances of getting free publicity multiply.

How to know what an editor wants

Editors do not guess about what interests their readers. Editors know what interests their readers. With years of accumulated experience, and files of data filled with tried and tested results, editors know what does and does not please their readers. Editors know their readers want news items that are unique and pleasing to their self-interest. Readers also do not want daily, weekly, or monthly repeats of the same old thing. They want fresh and original material. Something stimulating, something new.

Your job is to sit down and brainstorm. You must present your strongest benefits and advantages in your message, but you also should try to find a unique twist, angle, or hook that catches, and keeps, readers' attention. What you have to say must be branded in their minds, and create the desire to know more.

CAUTION If your tone is condescending or arrogant, no one will listen to you.

note

You must write your copy as if you were speaking directly to the reader. You will tell that person something of interest, and you want to make him/her listen. You must speak in a clear and understandable voice. You must be confident and friendly, professional but approachable. And, above all, you must use words that an average person would use in a one-on-one conversation. Once you achieved the feeling of communicating with a person on that level, you are ready to write your news release.

note Readers want interesting, factual, and useful information, and that is what you must present to them in your press release.

The editor knows what his/her readers can relate to. By examining the contents of publications, you also will. Getting the editor's attention may be easier than you think, if you know ahead of time what gets a readers attention. Generally, they are one and the same.

Writing a news release

A news release should not be written like an ad. Remember, what you are writing is not an "ad" release, but a "news" release. It should contain news. No-one buys a magazine to read ads. You pay for the privilege of placing an ad in a publication, and then write copy to compete, not only with other ads, but with the articles that appear. People read informational news first. Ads are generally the furthest thing from their minds until they see one that catches their eye. That is where your news release has an advantage. People read your publicity simply because it is news.

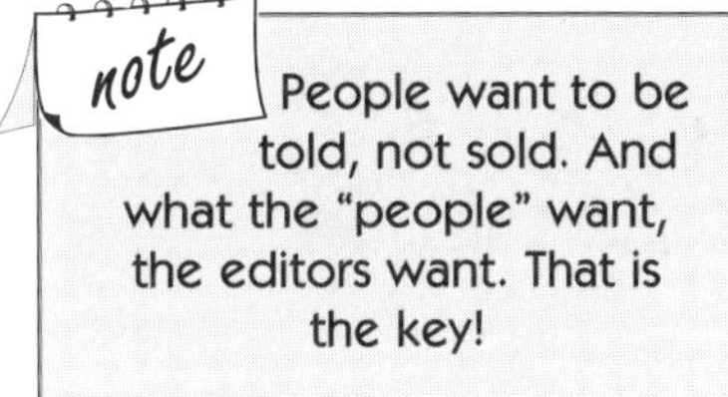

When you write your news release, talk more about the benefits and advantages of your product rather than the product. Leave the impression that you are concerned about what the product can do for the reader. Target the reader's self-interest, and avoid the thought that you are trying to sell a product. If your news release appears to be an ad, it will not be accepted as being a release.

News release format guidelines

The basic news release format guidelines are as follows:

1) Centered, capitalized, and underlined, type the words PRESS RELEASE: approximately 1.5 inches from the top of a plain piece of 8.5x11 paper. Immediately following the colon, enter a date. If it is for immediate release, enter the words For Immediate Release.

2) On the same line as your PRESS RELEASE: heading, go to the far left side of the paper, and type FOR FURTHER INFORMATION CONTACT: On the following lines enter your name, address, telephone number, and Fax number.

3) Center and enter your headline in bold print from a third to half way down the first page. Space two to four lines, and start your release.

4) Double space your lines, type on one side only, and limit your release to two pages. Do not staple the pages together. You must capture the interest, and involve the reader in the first paragraph of your release.

5) Use no more than three or four short sentences that immediately express the important facts of your story. Editors want to know "Who, What, When, Where, and Why." Editors receive many news releases and know almost at a glance if one has any potential. Always start your story with the most important information, and progress to the least important. Make your story stand out in a way that makes the reader stop and take notice.

> note
>
> Newspapers are very protective of their reputations. Make certain your story is honest, accurate, and believable.

After you write your release, go over it carefully and eliminate words like "I", "and," "an," and "the." Do not write first-person copy.

The main things to remember when you write your news release are that it must be interesting to the readers, be newsworthy, written in a style that is compatible with the publication's, typed and double spaced, and as brief as possible.

Press release packages

Many news releases never make it past an editor's desk because they are poorly written, or something else is missing that might have gotten the editor's attention. A news release should be able to stand on its own, but it certainly would not be a distraction to include an eye-catcher in your press package.

An 8x10 colored photograph would certainly make anyone take notice, but that may be overdoing it a bit. Not to mention the photo, packaging, and postage expenses involved. A 4x5 black-and-white works just as well in getting the attention you want. It is less expensive to produce, and can be mailed in a standard No. 10 envelope. Do not go second class with your photograph. Do not try to cut corners when you are trying to make an impression. It does not work.

If you have a brochure, include it in your package along with your *Press Release Response Request Form.* And, include a brief cover letter written to the individual that will review your package. If you do not know who that will be, find out. Call or write to the publication and ask who is responsible. You should be able to get this information, however, just by referring to the publication. Do not send your package or cover letter to some anonymous person; personalize it by going directly to the source.

Press release response request form

A press release response form should be included with every package you mail. The purpose of the form is to produce instant feedback, and to tell you if the publisher is interested in your release. Many people wait for weeks or even months, wondering if their release will appear. By providing a response request form, along with your self addressed, stamped envelope, you may know in a matter of days if the publications are interested.

Feature stories and book reviews

Another excellent source for free publicity can be found in feature stories and book reviews. They are less confining than a news release, and the reporter who does a feature story on you and your product has a great deal more flexibility in the style, format, and information that can be included.

Do not ever pass up the chance to have a reporter do a feature article on your business. A lengthy article, written by a professional, attracts even more attention than a two- or three-paragraph news release. A reporter also knows how to make a story interesting, and usually comes up with angles you may have overlooked that serves to promote your product. Reporters always are looking for interesting subjects to write about. If your story is interesting, all you have to do is make the right connection.

Prepublication background information

How do reporters find feature stories to write on? They follow up leads. Once they make contact, they complete a prepublication background report to determine if the event, story, etc., is newsworthy. But, you can provide a great service to yourself and a reporter by submitting your own background information for feature story consideration.

A *prepublication background information* format is an alternative to a news release. Its purpose is to get the attention of the reporter whose interests are basically the same as the editor's. The bottom line, as always, is "will it serve the interests of our readers?"

So what does interest their readers? The best way to find out is to read the publication to see what the reporter you will contact writes about. Some specialize in certain areas, and if you can tie your product in with a reporter's general theme, you increase your chances of getting into print.

Your background information should include essential information, but be constructed in a loose format. Then, add in all the necessary details. You do not have to get too wordy. If you have an interesting story to tell that you feel would enhance a reader's interest, summarize it. The reporter will ask for further details.

note

Your background submission should not exceed two or three pages. If you have other items to submit, such as diagrams, charts, statistical information, histories, testimonials, or copies of previous news stories, include them in an appendix.

A background information format must accomplish two things: It must generate enough interest to convince a reporter that your story is newsworthy, and interesting to the publication's readers. And, two, it must provide a reporter with enough information to make a preliminary decision to write about whatever it is you want publicized.

> note
>
> Your background submission provides an informational outline from which a reporter determines if an interesting and informative article can be written.

The format that is used most often is simple and easy to understand.

1) Indicate who the reporter should contact, including your name, address, and home and office telephone numbers.
2) Indicate a story title such as, "Local Author Writes Best Seller," or "Entrepreneur Opens New Business," etc. Then, briefly tell your story.
3) Tell the reporter who would be interested and why they would benefit from what you have to publicize.
4) Briefly tell any interesting or unique facts about your product, business, etc.
5) Include an appendix if you have any supplemental data.

Book reviews

If you have a book to sell, a book review is an effective way to get free publicity and sales. There are two approaches to pursue with book reviews: the prepublication review and the postpublication review.

Prepublication reviews

Prepublication reviews are particularly important for the book industry. Many publications review a book prior to its publication, which in turn allows bookstores the opportunity to place orders and have the book in stock before customers start requesting copies.

> *note* Prepublication reviews serve and direct their findings toward the book trade.

If your book is a new release, you should send copies of your book (or bound photocopies of the pasted boards), along with a cover letter, reply card, news release, and any other pertinent information, to any of the following publications, at least 90 days before your book is to be published and released.

Your cover letter should be addressed to the attention of the *Book Review Editor* (unless noted below). In your letter, introduce the title of your book, give a brief description of its contents, state how readers benefits from the information, tell the editor you are hopeful that he/she will enjoy the book, and thank him/her for his/her time and consideration.

- **American Library Association,** Attn: Up Front Editor, 50 East Huron St, Chicago, IL 60611. This particular magazine is directed at libraries.

- **Association of College and Research Libraries,** American Library Association, 100 Riverview Center, Middletown, CT 06457. Undergraduate school libraries are covered by this magazine.

- **Library Journal**, Attn: Book Reviews, 205 E, 42nd St, New York, NY 10017. This magazine's specialty is reviewing nonfiction.
- **Los Angeles Times Magazine,** Attn: Book Review Editor, Times-Mirror Square, Los Angeles, CA 90053.
- **The New York Times,** Attn: Daily Book Page, 229 West 43rd St, New York, NY 10036.
- **Publishers Weekly,** Attn: Forecasts Editor, 205 E. 42nd St, New York, NY 10017. Bookstore owners want to know how a book will be promoted and distributed to ensure that they have customers interested in buying your book. Include the appropriate information.
- **The Washington Post,** Book World, 1150 15th St, NW, Washington, D.C. 20071.

Postpublication book reviews

Book reviewers who work for major newspapers and magazines offer an effective way of obtaining free publicity for a book. Together, they review hundreds of books every week. The majority of books they receive, however, are not reviewed. The main reason why many books never receive a second look is because the accompanying press package (if there even was one) did not generate any interest. Book reviewers are busy people, and there is no shortage of work for them to do, and the stack tray is constantly replenished. Still, they may review two or three dozen book in a single workweek. If you want your press package to be read, make it grab their attention, but also make it short and to the point.

To save yourself a lot of time and expense, send your review package to those magazines that target the type of readers your book is geared to, as we already discussed in this report. Determine which targeted group is most likely be interested in your book, and target magazines that also appeal to that select group.

Postpublication request form

A Postpublication Request Form should be included with your review package. The purpose, as with a press release, is to get instant feedback from a reviewer. Be sure to include a self-addressed, postage-paid envelope. It is not necessary to send your book with your package. That practice could become very costly. If a reviewer is interested, he/she will request a sample, using the Postpublication Request Form you provided.

Generally speaking, however, a review package will consist of your book or photograph of the book, a news-release type review, a cover letter, and your request form. How your review is written is extremely important, because some reviewers may allow your release to be printed exactly the way it was written.

> *note* The purpose of your cover letter is to excite the reviewer and get him/her interested.

Free publicity

There are literally thousands of newspapers and magazines in the United States, many of which are highly specialized and geared to specific groups of people. In addition to offering great sources of advertising, they also offer unlimited potential for editorial mention and free publicity. All you have to do is convince them that your product, topic, idea, or service will be well received by their readers.

Editors and reportes always are looking for interesting news and feature stories. You do not have to be a great writer, but what you write about must offer news-type interest. If your product, idea, story, etc., has merit and shows some potential, an editor or reporter can take it from there and rewrite it to their customers' satisfaction.

The following randomly picked publications were taken from the *Directory of Leading Magazines and Newspapers* described in this report. There are thousands of magazines and newspapers that actively look for products, ideas, books, services, and programs to publicize for the benefit of their readers. If what you want publicized is interesting, unusual, unique, or different, then these publications will be interested in hearing from you.

- *Advertising Age*, Crain Communications, Inc., 740 Rush St, Chicago, IL 60611. 84,000 weekly. Display and classifieds.

- *Better Homes and Gardens*, Locust at 17th St, Des Moines, IA 50336. 8,000,000 monthly. Display only.

- *Boating*, CBS Publications, 1515 Broadway, New York, NY 10036. 190,000 monthly. Display and classified.

- *Cappers Weekly*, 616 Jefferson St, Topeka, KS 66607. 400,000 biweekly. Display and classified.

- *Direct Marketing Magazine*, Hoke Communications, Inc., 224 Seventh St, Garden City, NY 11530. 15,000 monthly. Display and classified.

- *Entrepreneur Magazine*, 2311 Pontius Avenue, Los Angeles, CA 90064. 190,000 monthly. Display only.

- *Glamour*, 350 Madison Avenue, New York, NY 10017, 2,225,000 monthly. Display only.

- *Grit*, 208 W. 3rd St, Williamsport, PA 17701. 600,000 weekly. Display and classified.

- *House and Garden*, 350 Madison Avenue, New York, NY 10017. 650,000 monthly, ten times per year. Display only.
- *Mademoiselle*, 350 Madison Avenue, New York, NY 10017. 1,000,000 monthly. Display only.
- *The Globe*, 5401 NW Broken Sound Blvd, Boca Raton, FL 33487. 1,100,000 weekly. Display and classified.
- *Parade*, 750 Third Avenue, New York, NY 10017. 30,500,000 weekly. Display only.
- *Popular Communications*, 76 N. Broadway, Hicksville, Ny 10003. 220,000 monthly. Display only.
- *Southern Living*, 820 Shades Creek Parkway, Birmingham, AL 35209 2,212,000 monthly. Display only.
- *The Star*, 660 White Plains Rd, Tarry Town, NY 10591. 3,600,000 weekly. Display and classified.
- *The Russ von Hoelscher Direct Response Profit Report*, Publisher Media, PO Box 546, El Cajon, CA 92022. No advertising.

Newsletters

There are thousands of newsletters that represent millions of subscribers. Their special interest groups include everything from direct-response marketers and investors, to antique collectors and sports enthusiasts. Many of them will print your entire news release and/or article free of charge. For a complete listing, refer to *The Newsletter Yearbook Directory* at your local library. If they don't have it, write to:

Newsletter Clearing House, 44 West Market St, Rhinebeck, NY 12572

Per-inquiry advertising

Contact nine out of ten broadcasters, and ask them if they are interested in per-inquiry advertising, and they will say "no." If you accept that as a final answer you have a long way to go in the business world. Some broadcasters will not have the slightest idea what you are talking about, and it has to be explained to them. Others say "no" because they do not want to eliminate the possibility that you will purchase some advertising.

So, here you come along and ask the manager of a radio or TV station for what basically amounts to free advertising. Naturally he/she will say "no," because if you want it bad enough you might pay for it anyway.

> note
>
> Do not let the broadcasters forget that you are ready to help them make money when they are not making money.

How do you handle that situation? Simple! Explain your product, the success you have had with it, how people want it, the benefits and advantages it will offer a listening or viewing audience, and how the broadcasters will make a percentage of profits for every product that is sold as a result of their advertising and promotional efforts.

If you cannot make an immediate deal (they may not have empty spots during peak season), leave your card and ask them to call when they can deal. If a few weeks go by and you have not heard from them, make a follow-up contact.

Simply put, *per-inquiry advertising* means you pay a broadcaster a certain agreed-on amount of your products that are sold. They have time to fill, you have something to advertise. If you can convince broadcasters that your product will sell, they will give you free air time. You pay per item sold. It is a money-making, and money-saving, proposition. While it reduces your risks as far as advertising costs, that is not, nor should it be, your primary purpose. You are in the business to make money.

Furthermore, the potential to make substantial gain for both parties is ever present. In fact, an advertiser stands to earn considerably more from your proposition that he/she would have selling advertisement. It is not guaranteed, of course, but the potential is there.

How per-inquiry advertising works

Per-inquiry advertisement agreements take place all the time, and in radio and television stations large and small. Independent television stations are more open to per-inquiry arrangements than larger network affiliates, and radio stations are more open to an agreement than TV stations. Marketers have had great success with smaller cable stations in late-night spots, where advertising is not sought after to the same degree as daytime programming.

Their part is to do the advertising, but you are expected to do all the fulfillment. You fill the orders and ship out the product. Honesty is an important factor in any negotiated agreement, and the best way to ensure trust is to assign a special address or box number where orders for your product may be sent. That allows a station to track all orders that result from its efforts.

If the station is responsible for picking up the mail, some stations will type pre-addressed shipping labels from the orders received. Others will simply forward the orders to you, and shipping labels will be your responsibility. Generally, the checks will accompany the orders and you would then pay the station the agreed-on percentage.

What percentage of profits will a station expect?

Most stations expect from one-half to three-quarters of the sale price. So, the question is, can you make a profit? For example: If you sell 200 books at $10 each, you make $2,000 in gross sales. If your agreement is on a 60/40 split (the station receives 60 percent), its share is $1,200. For every book you sell, it receives $6. If it handled all the receipts, it would send you $4.

If you are printing the book in large quantities, your costs including postage, may only represent $1.50 per book. Therefore, your net profit would be $2.50 per book, and you make a profit. Your profits in this conservative example are not enormous, but if you paid for the advertising (which you received free), you might not have made a profit at all! Just watch your profit margin in this type of arrangement. Do not enter into an agreement thinking you will get a price break from the printer, which you will pass on to the station before the fact, projecting that you receive 25,000 orders. But, if it does not go, the cash will flow, all in the wrong direction.

CAUTION

When the orders do start to come in, establish your reliability and credibility with fast service. If customers begin to complain that their orders are not being received, your free advertising will be over. Also, do not try to pull a fast one by suddenly inflating the price on your product in an effort to increase your profit margin. Stations are well aware of what a fair price is. The last thing they will do is help you make more money at the expense of their listening or viewing audience.

note

If you sell yourself and your product to the directors, then they will sell your product also, through free advertising.

When you meet with any radio or television advertising director, go prepared! Make up a professional sales package that includes a news release, photos, testimonials, news articles, press releases, cover letter, and anything else that will enhance the image of you and your product. "The proof is in the pudding," or in this case, your sales package.

Publications and per-inquiry advertising

Most publications, large or small, are open to a per-inquiry advertising agreement, and the profit split arrangements are much the same as radio and television per-inquiry advertising. Publications will advertise your product for you at no charge, for a percentage of the sales. This arrangement not only helps fill empty space, but it is something of a challenge and ego trip for them, in that it represents an opportunity to test how well an advertisement pulls in the publication. They also assume that, if profits are substantial after one or two issues, you the provider will determine that it may be advantageous to become a paying advertiser. And you may just agree with that thinking, especially if the profits exceed the cost of an ad.

> **note** Publications often enter into a per-inquiry agreement just to show a provider that advertising with them does not mean taking a risk, but making profits.

If your product is books, mail-order publishing houses also will agree to some per-inquiry agreements. When an established mail-order house advertises your product in its catalog, you gain instant credibility. It already has established a reputation of trust and dependability with its customers, and your product benefits from what can be considered no less than a powerful advertising tool. Send your sales package to mail-order houses that appear to have items in their catalog compatible with what you are selling. If they accept your offer, consider yourself very fortunate. Sales will be made.

Be enthusiastic and persistent

Never lose your enthusiasm when you approach a broadcaster or publisher with your per-inquiry proposition. Enthusiasm is contagious. It has a way of making good impressions, and creating lasting working relationships. Few business people will ever walk up to you, out of the blue, and offer you a per-inquiry advertising deal. Understandably, they are in the business of selling advertising, not giving it away. Understand that fact, but also use friendly persuasion. A combination of humility, professionalism, enthusiasm, and persistence can turn a hard-nosed pessimist into a believer.

Left over space

A publication's worst nightmare is that it will go to press with left over space, or *remnant space*. The print and broadcast media have deadlines that must be met. When it becomes obvious that there will be some unfilled space, marketing directors suddenly becomes more susceptible to allowing you to buy advertising space, not at 17 percent, but at up to 50 percent, or even more. They will of course make this offer to established customers, who for one reason or another are not advertising in that particular issue, but that should not distract you from letting the marketing directors know you have an ad, that you intend to be a regular, and that you would appreciate the same consideration they give any other established customer.

In effect, what you are requesting is the "*standby advertising rate*." If you ask marketing directors to run your ad on a standby-rate basis only, that means that it is run only if there is unused space that must be filled. As that situation arises (and it happens regularly), you then enjoy the discounted rate. If nothing is available when you request it, let the editor or marketing director know that you would like to have your ad run if a standby opportunity should arise, whether in the near or distant future. That type of flexibility puts you in the forefront of their minds, and they will not have to make a lot of unnecessary follow-up phone calls to see if an advertiser who was interested one week, is still interested the next.

"Till-forbid" advertising

A *till-forbid* advertising discount occurs if you allow your ad to run consistently in a certain number of issues. For example, one run may cost you $200; five runs, $185; and ten runs, $160 per issue. This is not free advertising, but you should at least be aware of the various discounts that can save you money. In the example described above, you would receive $400 worth of free advertising if you ran your ad in ten consecutive issues.

Till-forbid advertising does not mean that you are locked in by a contract and must run your ad ten times. It means that you told the magazine, etc., to run your ad until you advise it/them to stop. If you stop after six issues, you then receive the six-issue rate. When you are negotiating for advertising rates with the editor of a magazine with nothing better to offer at the time, and you feel that it is wise to get into the magazine as soon as possible, then ask for their till-forbid rates.

Co-op advertising

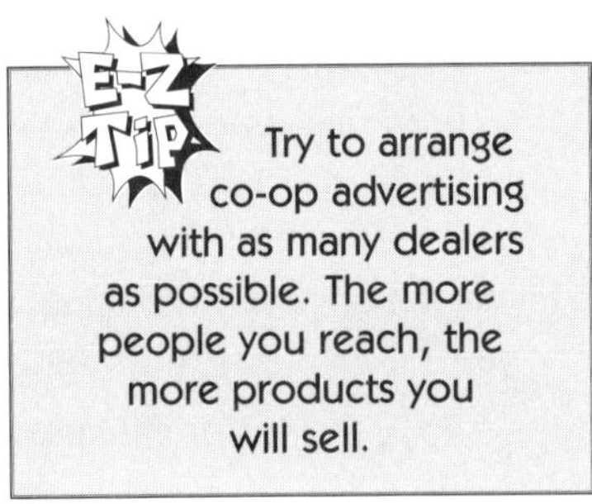

Thousands of mail-order dealers sell advertising space that is placed onto circulars or in catalogs, newsletters, and other publications. Because they are in the same business you are and are targeting the same buying audience, swapping space would benefit all parties involved. For example, you could swap equal sized ads, or an ad for mailing out a certain number of a dealer's circulars. This type of arrangement can create profitable opportunities in that each party can reach thousands of prospects in a cooperative swap advertising or other resources, agreement. But, do not think in terms of single deals. Make certain however that the dealer you swap with has a publication and targeted audience that is compatible with what you are offering. Advertising swaps mean nothing if you reach 50,000 people who are not interested in your offer.

If a dealer does not sell advertising space, offer to exchange other sales literature or envelope stuffers. He/she mails out 5,000 of your circulars in a mailing campaign, and you insert 5,000 of his/hers. The object is to reach people other than those currently on your mailing list. Naturally, you do not want to enter this type of arrangement with a dealer who is in direct competition with you, with the same products, for example. But, those dealers offering similar products represent your best prospects. That ensures that your offer is reaching the most likely buyers.

Swap ad space for articles

Most mail-order publications, including magazines and newsletters, actively solicit articles that enhance every issue and provide information that would interest their readers. If you can write feature articles, this is yet another opportunity to trade off your expertise for free or reduced ad space.

A published article can be valuable to you even if ad space is not a part of the deal. Your article can still produce direct inquiries. For example, you wrote book about some specialized area of direct-response mailing. Your story could focus on the subject, and in your close you simply mention where people could write to receive additional information, or purchase, your book.

If you can write interesting articles that tie in with the interest of a publisher's targeted reading audience, you can make trade-off deals that benefit you and a publisher. Write four to six different articles and submit them along with a cover letter describing your proposal. Sell the publisher on the fact that you are recognized as an authority in your field of expertise. If you are a mail-order authority, author, copywriter, etc., say so. Be specific. If you are the author of 15 books, one of which sold well, say so. Be specific when it is in your best interest. Do not make claims, however, that you cannot substantiate.

E-Z TIP

Make it clear that you don't expect any pay for submitting your articles, but you do want full credit and want your inquiry solicitation included at the end of your article. This type of trade-off advertising is done by thousands of writers and publishers every day. By sending copies of three to four, or more, different articles, a publisher can stagger your articles over six months or a year. Sending one article at a time would involve too much time and expense for you and a publisher. This method of advertising can provide you with publicity that can reach hundreds of thousands of prospects, many of whom may become customers.

Mail-order catalog advertising

Mail-order catalog advertising can offer you great sales and publicity opportunities. If you have a book or product to sell, write to mail-order companies for additional information on free catalog house listings.

> **note** A catalog house will usually ask for a 50 to 70 percent cut.

Catalog houses reach millions of people with their catalogs. When you write to a catalog house, send them your promotional package, complete with a cover letter, fact sheet regarding your product, suggested retail price, 4x5 photograph, copy of your proposed ad, testimonials, and any other sales literature that enhances your offer. If they decide to advertise your product, consider yourself very fortunate. Catalog Houses are very effective in selling products through the mail to millions of new and established customers.

Free radio and television publicity

As we briefly discussed, the purpose of publicity is to inform readers, listeners or viewers, and not to sell. This is the one area where editors and directors allow their audiences to be told, but not sold. Selling is advertising, and that is where they draw the line. They allow you to have free publicity because it is news, and the fact that you want to sell something to their audiences is not their concern. They already know that is your purpose, they just do not want it to be obvious. Free publicity is an effective way to generate interest and sales for your product.

> *note* Radio and television stations are constantly looking for stories to put on the air.

Whether consciously or subconsciously, research has shown that people welcome interesting, down-to-earth stories that gives them a break from distressing, sensationalistic, trauma-type news that is forced upon them 24 hours a day. To give people a break, radio and TV stations insert human interest feature stories. They give people a chance to relax, and perhaps restore their faith in humanity as a whole.

The feature story may be about unique quilt making, someone who dedicated his/her life to helping others, a person who finds a briefcase filled with cash and turns it in to the authorities, or someone who wrote a book that benefits others in some manner.

Just watch any television news program or listen to your favorite radio broadcaster, and you will discover that they always air a human-interest feature story. All news does not have to be depressing, and the stations make certain it is not.

Creating interest is the key to free publicity

Because radio and television stations must appeal to a mass viewing and listening audience, all of whom have a diversified interest, they are constantly looking for news that appeals to their broad audience. That appeal may involve featuring a story on any of a thousand subjects, but the one basic ingredient that subject must have is *interest.*

> **CAUTION** An editor will see through any attempt to get free advertising. What you are looking for is free publicity.

Anyone who is capable of being creative to the extent of turning an interesting business and product into a feature story that interests viewers and listeners can exploit the vast opportunities in the powerful broadcast industry. From just one simple, but unique, human-interest angle, you reap the rewards of what can often be unaffordable advertising.

The one thing to remember is that the job of a broadcaster is to entertain. You can create a mutually beneficial situation by developing a story that contains interesting news. It may be humorous or serious, but it must deliver a story that appeals to a large segment of the broadcaster's audience. But, do not think in terms of making a commercial. If you do, it will be extremely difficult to get a suggested feature story past an editor.

Reaching a targeted audience

Because there are more radio stations than television stations, it is much easier to get targeted publicity on radio programs. Television, by its very nature, exposes its programming to a more general audience. That makes it difficult to target a specific audience. However, radio talk shows target a multitude of special interest groups, from child psychology to gardening. There are radio programs that target farmers, homemakers, children, young adults who prefer rock to country, and blue-collar workers who prefer country to rock, and still others who prefer classical music. The audiences are more defined.

When you know what format a radio broadcast is designed for, you can target that specific audience to your full advantage. If you can somehow tie your product in with the interests of a specific special interest group, then you are close to accomplishing something great in your marketing strategies. You have to know your product, of course, and who it appeals to best. As we previously discussed, the best place to start is with a paper and pencil. Write down every benefit and advantage your product has to offer, then write a news release that focuses on the most powerful, appeal points of your product. Only then will you know for certain who your most likely prospects will be.

There is no easy way to determine what the format of every station's programming is in the United States. The *Standard Rates and Data Directory* (available at your library) lists all the radio stations, and tells you if they are talk shows or what kind of music they provide, but that is the extent of it. The only way to find out is to determine which stations might somehow tie in with your product by "type of station" and then write to them for details.

When you hear from a station, and it appears to have the type of programming that suits your publicity, then send your publicity package. Whatever your story is, you must make it so interesting that it stands on its own merit when it comes to getting free air time. You have to find that unique angle that makes a broadcaster say, "Yes, this is what I've been looking for. I can't wait to get it on the air!"

Address your letter, photo, news release, copies of feature stories that appeared in print media, and any convincing news materials you included in your publicity package to the person that responded to your original inquiry. If it is not signed, or appears written by someone without decision-making authority, contact that person and find out who makes the final decision on your promotional package. That is the person you want to address your package to, no one else!

Test locally before going national

Before you send mass mailings on a national level, it is best to test your promotional package on a local level. You will not have to research the *Standard Rates and Data Directory* to get that information. Just check your local newspaper for a complete listing of all radio and television stations that are serving your area. List the talk, news, music, etc., shows, especially those that have an ongoing format that deals with local interests, and start making your contacts.

When you make your first contact, remember Rule No. 1: Do not tell the person that you are trying to promote a product. What you have is an interesting story. They want a story filled with information that will be entertaining; think of what would make your story unique and interesting, and then tie in your product. If your story is interesting and has some convincing appeal that a producer, director, reporter, etc., takes a personal interest in, you are home free. If you want publicity such as live radio and TV interviews, you have to sell yourself as well as your story. They are often one and the same when it comes down to live interviews. A human-interest story (especially on TV) may require a live appearance, even if it is just a single comment as a part of the feature that has was produced. Chances are you will not have a rehearsal, so

Once again remember, "They want to Tell, not Sell," when it comes to publicity.

be prepared when the opportunity presents itself. Formulate your comments for maximum impressions and publicity impact.

Preparing also means dressing appropriately, communicating clearly, arriving at the studio at the time you are asked to be there, practicing answers to every possible question you could be asked, and presenting a pleasant and professional personality. The following tips will help you overcome any interview jitters.

- *Be confident*: Remove any negative thoughts about your ability to conduct a good interview by planning ahead. Planning instills self-confidence.

- *Interview yourself*: Write down every conceivable question an interviewer might ask on the topic you will be interviewed about. Have someone else throw the questions at you, and imagine you are on the air at that moment.

- *Avoid the unavoidable*: An interviewer may ask a few questions in an area that you have no expertise. Do not get into a position where you start tripping over your own feet. Be honest. If you cannot come up with an answer that is intelligent, politely pass.

- *"Smile, you're on Candid Camera!"* Forget about the cameras. They are not people, they are not warm, and they will not congratulate you on a successful interview. Talk to the interviewer and concentrate on your discussions. When people get "stage fright," they sometimes fix their eyes on the very thing that frightens them and go into a trance. If that happens, you will be asking the interviewer to repeat every question and still will not know the answer.

- *When there is a pause, take the initiative*: A good interviewer will give you ample time to respond to questions. Do not interrupt half way into a question, you will not be playing "Name That Tune." When the appropriate pause comes, take the initiative and be in control of points you would like to make. Unless you are running for office, avoid getting into a debate.

If your story has something to do with becoming a clown, then it may be appropriate to dress as a clown. But, if your subject is about a more serious business-oriented topic, then dress like a competent and professional businessperson. People judge you by your appearance. Plan ahead. Ask the producer or director what colors, etc., look best on TV.

Have a feel for when the interview is about to end? That is your opportunity to summarize key points. Do not leave an audience hanging in those last few seconds. Do not assume that the interviewer will direct an audience to your doorstep. Let them know how and where you can be reached.

CAUTION

The best free publicity in the world is not worth a dime if you are not prepared to take advantage of it.

When the inquiries start coming in, be ready. Have your advertising literature printed up and ready to go to everyone who requests more information. Then, when the orders start to arrive, get them out fast! A happy customer is also a happy listener or viewer. What goes around, comes around. If your new customers are satisfied, you may just find yourself back in front of the TV cameras.

Regulated public service announcements

All radio and television stations in the United States are regulated by the Federal Communications Commission (FCC). Stations are licensed, and relicensed by the FCC based on the law and public service criteria.

Because the United States is "a government of the people, and for the people" in theory, the airways belong to the public. Therefore, for the privilege of using those airways, broadcasters are expected to provide a public service by means of free public service announcements that are in the public's interest. These announcements may include such things as a free blood pressure clinic, community-wide swimming lessons, a benefit supper to raise money for a volunteer fire department, or a bake sale to help a homeless family. Broadcasters are normally more than eager to announce nonprofit, fund-raising events, or make announcements that provide a service to the community as a whole. They then record their public service airway contributions and present them to the FCC as part of the relicensing procedure.

It is extremely difficult to get free publicity through free public service announcements. However, if you set up a nonprofit charity function you could tie in your product and receive indirect publicity. For example, your product could be the prize that is raffled off or given away as a door prize at a charitable event. Your product may not be the focal point of rolling cameras, but you as an organizer or primary participant certainly would. If you are prepared, you will be able to tie in your product somehow during an interview. It involves some of your time, but if done properly it could be well worth the effort.

If you want to take advantage of free public service announcements, send your fact sheet to broadcast stations far in advance of the event. This is your first opportunity to tie in with the event, so give all the facts not only about the event, but also who you are. Provide the stations with a clean, typed, and double-spaced letter that professionally describes the "who, what, when, where, and purpose" of the event.

Conclusion

No matter what type of business you are in, your success depends largely on your ability to use advertising and publicity to its full potential. You must be successful in marketing your product to make a profit. As you discovered in this report, advertising and publicity are obtainable, even for those who cannot afford it. The opportunity for free advertising and publicity is available to you, and they can be just as effective as any advertising that others are paying top dollar for.

Many new businesses fail because advertising costs consume what little money they may have had at the beginning. Free advertising and publicity can give you that initial boost that so many new businesses desperately need. If the only thing that has held you back from going into business for yourself is the cost of advertising, this report may have restored your enthusiasm. You will be an important step ahead of many others who have not yet discovered that it is not necessary to spend money on advertising and publicity. You now know how you can get it free.

E-Z TIP: Even after you have established yourself, and have funds that would allow you to buy top-dollar advertising, continue to use free advertising and publicity to an even greater degree.

To get started on your business road to success, invest your time in news releases and make a concerted attempt to get stories that feature you and your product published. Get all the free publicity and advertising that is available. As you begin to enjoy profits, you then develop an advertising budget that can boost you toward even greater goals.

If you multiply your success ten time over, increase your efforts parallel to your success. With success comes confidence, with confidence, enthusiasm. Together they create a believable credibility factor that somehow makes people want to be associated with you. To put it simply, the more successful you become, the easier it is to obtain free advertising and publicity.

People tend to forget that basic success factor. Influence is a by-product of success. A modest business beginning may not lend itself to the compelling power of influence, but each step forward enhances your sphere of influence. The more you have, the more they give. Become a celebrity within your own field, and broadcasters will contact you. It may sound incredible, but it is true! If you advertised and publicized yourself, for example, as a person who everyone in the publishing and broadcast media wants to interview, you build a reputation as a much sought-after figure who obviously, by virtue of all the publicity, has something to offer. Who would turn you down if you offered your time? It works the same with a product. Use the power of the media for all it is worth. And your worth will soar!

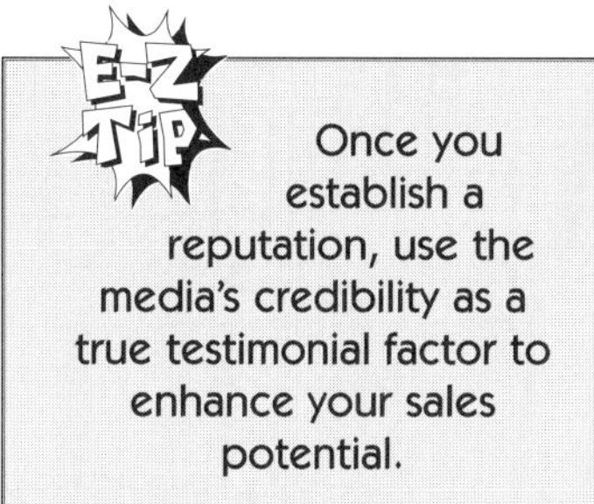

BONUS: The Dirty Little Secret About Market Research That No One Ever Talks About

The Dirty Little Secret About Market Research That No One Ever Talks About

© 1994 Jonathan Mizel (Reprinted with permission.)

There is an incredibly dirty little secret about market research almost nobody ever talks about. And that secret is this:

No one does it!

That's right. Almost nobody who is trying to sell a product or service does any meaningful market research at all. Now I'm not talking about expensive customer interviews or costly focus groups that the big ad agencies perform. I'm talking about low-cost or no-cost methods of obtaining crucial information about your customers that can dramatically improve your chances of selling to them.

Let me give you an example: Have you ever known anyone who produced an informational product (audio, video, report, etc.) that didn't sell very well? Of course you have. The main reason these types of projects fail is because people do not research their market properly.

You see, everyone says that they do market research on their target audience, but do you know what? Ninety-nine times out of a hundred, people have absolutely no idea who their customers really are. When I begin working with people as their copywriting/advertising consultant, I always ask them what type of market research they have done.

Their answers are usually something like this: "My mother loves it," "My girlfriend thinks this is the best tape ever," or the worse, "The man who sold me the ad down at the newspaper said my video is gonna sell like crazy!"

While other people's opinions are not completely baseless, they are not especially helpful. In fact, they can even be dangerous if taken at face value.

Remember, the only opinion that really counts is that of your customer!

Here are three very simple things you can do right now that will immediately put your market research on overdrive:

1) Send out a survey or questionnaire to your existing customers asking for four things:

   - First of all, ask them general questions about their age, marital status, do they own their own home, which credit cards do they prefer using, etc.

   - Second, ask them to rate your product on a 1 - 10 scale and have them offer suggestions on improving or modifying it. (Make sure you tell them to be completely honest.)

   - Third, ask them for comments and/or testimonials that you can use in future marketing endeavors. (I usually suggest adding this at the end of the survey: "Please check here if we may use your comments in our advertising materials.")

   - And finally, ask them for the names, addresses, and phone numbers of three other people who would be interested in receiving information about your products.

2) Complete a customer profile on your target audience (the people you would like as customers in the future). Your customer profile should include such things as age, gender, income, education, etc. This little

exercise will establish three things that, though they may seem obvious at first, are essential to successful marketing and are often overlooked:

a) The profile will determine whether your target is even worth pursuing as a market (for example, if your target audience isn't employed, or if they don't have credit cards, you should probably scrap the project).

b) It will tell you which media to use to approach them (direct mail, radio, newspapers, billboards, newsletters, space advertisements, computer bulletin boards, etc.).

c) And finally, it will help you formulate your offer and give you insight into how to sell to your market.

3) Go to the library and pull a copy of the *Standard Rate and Data Service Mailing List Directory (SRDS).* Look for mailing lists available under the subject matter that pertains to your product to determine five things:

- Are your potential customers available in list form from a list broker or competitor?
- What media methods do your potential customers respond best to (direct-mail, space ads, television, etc.)?
- How much are people willing to pay for a similar product or service?
- How do existing customers prefer to pay for their purchases?
- What is the general demographic makeup of your target market?

By using these simple and highly effective methods of market research and customer identification, you can save a lot of time and hassle. Especially if you perform them before you create your product or expand your product line.

Marketing is not luck or even magic. Marketing is simply determining who your customer is, deciding how to approach them, and finally, knowing what to say to them that will make them buy!

P.S. Attached please find the customer profile I use along with instructions. It lists 30 things to ask yourself before you start any marketing project.

How to use the Customer Profile Worksheet

The attached *Customer Profile Worksheet* was initially developed in 1991. In trying to understand why certain projects did well while others failed miserably, I realized that the formula for success had almost nothing to do with my product. The formula for success almost completely had to do with my market.

Therefore, I decided the best thing to do was to try understand and define exactly who my market was before I spent any money testing advertisements or direct mail pieces. I wanted to get a very clear mental picture of who my customer was. What they physically looked like. Their wants, needs, and desires. The reasons why are as follows:

- It is important to determine whether the potential market you are going after has the makings of a good customer base. In other words, do they have good income, steady employment, available credit, and are they open to purchasing goods and services through direct-marketing methods?

- If they are indeed good customers, which methods are best used to approach them. What do they read, watch on television, etc.? Would they be open to an ad in *Soap Opera Digest*, or did they need a personal letter sent to them via Federal Express before they respond to an offer? Did they watch MTV, read technical newsletters, or subscribe to *The Globe*? In other words, which media were they exposed to regularly.

- Finally, one then needs to figure out which offers they would respond to best. Do they mind spending $250 for three video tapes on fly-fishing? Would they prefer paying in installments? Are they motivated by "fear of loss," or "chance of gain?" What was their pain level, and how could I solve their problem best?

There are three uses for this profile.

1) First of all, use it to profile your existing customer base. Find out who they are and what they are all about (their basic demographics).

2) Second, use it to profile your potential customers. The people you are going after as new customers (see explanation above).

3) Finally, just for fun, complete a profile on your dream customers. Those who make $250,000 a year, own Ferraris, went to graduate school, and buy virtually everything they own through the mail, etc. One word of caution: If your dream customers are totally different from your existing customers, it usually means that you failed to perform proper market research before you began your project. (Don't worry, now that you are armed with the profile and instructions for using it, you will never again have to waste money on useless tests.)

As you complete the profile, almost everything is self-explanatory. There are, however, three items that may need some clarification: numbers #17, #18, and #30. Here are answers to some of the common queries I receive regarding these, along with my reasons for the necessity of compiling this information in the first place:

- **#17 Intelligence level:** Base this on a scale of 1 to 3 (with 1 being the lowest). This item is important because it will help you when you formulate your offer. While it is never a good idea to complicate your advertisements, be extra careful to keep your offers to the '1s as simple as possible.

  Also, avoid using words or phrases that are difficult to understand or are not in common everyday language. I usually recommend keeping your ad copy to about a 7th or 8th grade level for those people who are not overly educated. Even in the best case scenarios (professionals, attorneys, doctors, etc.), never go over a 9th or 10th grade reading level when writing ad copy (you can easily check this on your computer if you have a grammar checking feature).

- **#18 Culture Quotient:** Again, use a 1 to 3 scale based on the highest level of the potential media your customers are exposed to. A "1" would be the tabloids, comic books, and television. A "2" would be movies, newspapers and fiction novels. A "3" would be the symphony, opera, ballet, theater, museums, and non-fiction technical books.

  I'm not saying a "3" is better than a "1" or trying to be snobbish in any way. It's just that we need that clear mental picture of our customer before we begin the project. After all, if you were selling a video on something like "how to improve your golf game," the culture quotient could come in handy when you were planning and buying your media. (For example, would you rather run an ad in the True Detective, or in this season's symphony program?)

- **#30 Do they stay current?:** This is essential to know if you are trying to use a timely headline or other contemporary sales angle. For example, right now, NAFTA (the North American Free Trade Agreement) is very big in the news. So is gun control, health care, the information superhighway, and the upcoming elections. You may wish to exploit these issues if you can to make more sales. Using a timely headline or sales pitch can be extremely effective, but only if the people you are making an offer to stay current enough to know what you are talking about.

Use the profile in every marketing or selling situation. Know your customer and it's much easier to sell them.

(See next page for customer profile worksheet)

Customer Profile Worksheet

Project Name______________________________

Client Name_______________________________

1. Age:
2. Gender:
3. Income:
4. Education:
5. Occupation:
6. Married?:
7. Kids - How Many?:
8. Own a Telephone?:
9. Own a Television?:
10. Own a VCR?:
11. Have a Credit Card?:
12. Good Overall Credit?:
13. Own a Home?:
14. Own a Car - What Kind?:
15. Race:
16. Religion:
17. Intelligence Level:
18. Culture Quotient:
19. Own a Computer?:
20. Own a Modem?:
21. Hobbies:
22. Own a Business?:
23. Political Affiliation:
24. Do They Commute - How?:
25. Do They Drink, Smoke, Drugs?:
26. Do They Open Own Mail?:
27. Do They Buy Through Mail?:
28. Regional Origin (South, Mid-west, Northeast, etc.):
29. Urban or Rural?:
30. Do They Stay Current?:
31. Do they Have Pets - What Kind?

Whatever you need to know, we've made it E-Z!

Informative text and forms you can fill out on-screen.* From personal to business, legal to leisure—we've made it E-Z!

PERSONAL & FAMILY

For all your family's needs, we have titles that will help keep you organized and guide you through most every aspect of your personal life.

BUSINESS

Whether you're starting from scratch with a home business or you just want to keep your corporate records in shape, we've got the programs for you.

* Not all topics include forms ss 1999.r2

FEDERAL & STATE Labor Law Posters

The Poster 15 Million Businesses Must Have This Year!

All businesses must display federal labor laws at each location, or risk fines and penalties of up to $7,000! And changes in September and October of 1997 made all previous Federal Labor Law Posters obsolete; so make sure you're in compliance—use ours!

State	Item#
Alabama	83801
Alaska	83802
Arizona	83803
Arkansas	83804
California	83805
Colorado	83806
Connecticut	83807
Delaware	83808
Florida	83809
Georgia	83810
Hawaii	83811
Idaho	83812
Illinois	83813
Indiana	83814
Iowa	83815
Kansas	83816
Kentucky	83817

State	Item#
Louisiana	83818
Maine	83819
Maryland	83820
Massachusetts	83821
Michigan	83822
Minnesota	83823
Mississippi	83824
Missouri	83825
Montana	83826
Nebraska	83827
Nevada	83828
New Hampshire	83829
New Jersey	83830
New Mexico	83831
New York	83832
North Carolina	83833
North Dakota	83834

State	Item#
Ohio	83835
Oklahoma	83836
Oregon	83837
Pennsylvania	83838
Rhode Island	83839
South Carolina	83840
South Dakota not available	
Tennessee	83842
Texas	83843
Utah	83844
Vermont	83845
Virginia	83846
Washington	83847
Washington, D.C.	83848
West Virginia	83849
Wisconsin	83850
Wyoming	83851

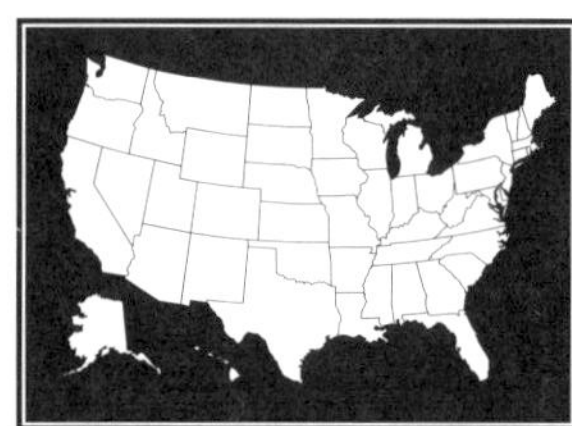

State Labor Law Compliance Poster

Avoid up to $10,000 in fines by posting the required State Labor Law Poster available from Made E-Z Products.

$29.95

Federal Labor Law Poster

This colorful, durable 17¾" x 24" poster is in full federal compliance and includes:

- The NEW Fair Labor Standards Act Effective October 1, 1996 (New Minimum Wage Act)
- The Family & Medical Leave Act of 1993*
- The Occupational Safety and Health Protection Act of 1970
- The Equal Opportunity Act
- The Employee Polygraph Protection Act

* Businesses with fewer than 50 employees should display reverse side of poster, which excludes this act.

$11.99
Stock No. LP001

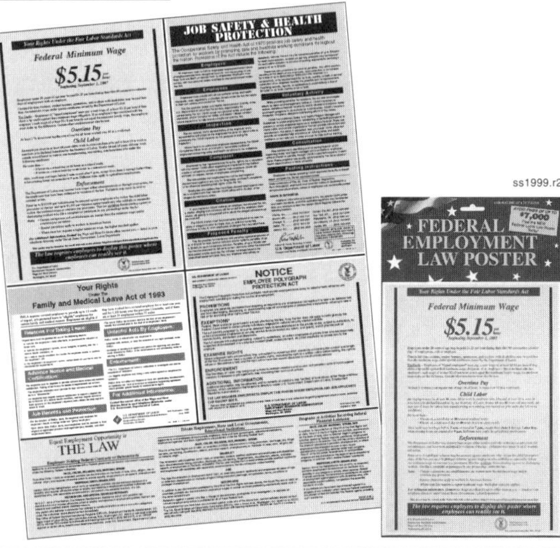

ss1999.r2

See the order form in this guide to order yours today!

CHECK OUT THE

MADE E·Z® LIBRARY

MADE E-Z GUIDES

Each comprehensive guide contains all the information you need to learn about one of dozens of topics, plus sample forms (if applicable).

Most guides also include an appendix of valuable resources, a handy glossary, and the valuable 14-page supplement "How to Save on Attorney Fees."

TITLES

Asset Protection Made E-Z
Shelter your property from financial disaster.

Bankruptcy Made E-Z
Take the confusion out of filing bankruptcy.

Buying/Selling a Business Made E-Z
Position your business and structure the deal for quick results.

Buying/Selling Your Home Made E-Z
Buy or sell your home for the right price right now!

Collecting Child Support Made E-Z
Ensure your kids the support they deserve.

Collecting Unpaid Bills Made E-Z
Get paid–and faster–every time.

Corporate Record Keeping Made E-Z
Minutes, resolutions, notices, and waivers for any corporation.

Credit Repair Made E-Z
All the tools to put you back on track.

Divorce Law Made E-Z
Learn to proceed on your own, without a lawyer.

Employment Law Made E-Z
A handy reference for employers and employees.

Everyday Law Made E-Z
Fast answers to 90% of your legal questions.

Everyday Legal Forms & Agreements Made E-Z
Personal and business protection for virtually any situation.

Incorporation Made E-Z
Information you need to get your company INC'ed.

Last Wills Made E-Z
Write a will the right way, the E-Z way.

Limited Liability Companies Made E-Z
Learn all about the hottest new business entity.

Living Trusts Made E-Z
Trust us to help you provide for your loved ones.

Living Wills Made E-Z
Take steps now to ensure Death with Dignity.

Managing Employees Made E-Z
Your own personnel director in a book.

Partnerships Made E-Z
Get your company started the right way.

Small Claims Court Made E-Z
Prepare for court...or explore other avenues.

Traffic Court Made E-Z
Learn your rights on the road and in court.

Solving IRS Problems Made E-Z
Settle with the IRS for pennies on the dollar.

Trademarks & Copyrights Made E-Z
How to obtain your own copyright or trademark.

Vital Record Keeping Made E-Z
Preserve vital records and important information.

KITS

Each kit includes a clear, concise instruction manual to help you understand your rights and obligations, plus all the information and sample forms you need.

For the busy do-it-yourselfer, it's quick, affordable, and it's E-Z.

ss 1999.r1

Index

A-Co•••••

Cr-F•••••

G-R•••••

Q-W•••••